LIKE FATHER, LIKE SON:
A FAMILY STORY

LIKE FATHER, LIKE SON: A FAMILY STORY

Michael Parkinson

with

Mike Parkinson

HODDER

First published in Great Britain in 2020 by Hodder & Stoughton
An Hachette UK company

This paperback edition published in 2021

1

A CIP catalogue record for this title is available from the British Library

Paperback ISBN 9781529362503
eBook ISBN 9781529362480

Typeset in Granjon by Hewer Text UK Ltd, Edinburgh
Printed and bound in Great Britain by Clays Ltd, Elcograf S.p.A.

Hodder & Stoughton policy is to use papers that are natural, renewable
and recyclable products and made from wood grown in sustainable
forests. The logging and manufacturing processes are expected to
conform to the environmental regulations of the country of origin.

Hodder & Stoughton Ltd
Carmelite House
50 Victoria Embankment
London EC4Y 0DZ

www.hodder.co.uk

This book is dedicated to
John William Parkinson, 1903–76,
Yorkshireman and miner.

CONTENTS

'The present is not . . . a hard line of demarcation between two opposite worlds, but a gentle mist through which they wander leisurely.'

Emile Cammaerts, 1930

PREFACE

To live in hearts we leave behind,
  Is not to die.

Thomas Campbell

*John William Parkinson: 'I only
hope they play cricket in heaven. If
they don't he'll ask for a transfer.'*

T HE PIECE BELOW IS A remembrance of my father that was
featured in a collection of my articles called *Parkinson's
Lore*, published in 1981. What I wrote then still sums up
what I feel about him today.

I was never told fairy tales as a child. Instead I heard
about Larwood's action and Hobbs's perfection. Before I
ever saw him play I knew Len Hutton intimately, and
the first time I witnessed Stanley Matthews in the flesh I
knew which way he was going even if the full-back
didn't. The stories of these gods, and many, many more
besides, I heard at my father's knee.

He was a remarkable man with a marvellous facility
to adorn an anecdote. It was he who invented the gate,
complete with attendant, which was built in honour of a
Barnsley winger who could run like the wind but didn't
know how to stop. At the end of one of his gallops the

gate would be opened and the winger would career through and out of the ground to finally come to a stop halfway across the car park. Or so Dad said.

It was he who told me of the full-back whose fearsome sliding tackles carried him into the wall surrounding the ground, causing the spectators to start wearing goggles at home games for fear of being blinded by flying chips of concrete. Frank Barson, he assured me, once ran the entire length of the field bouncing the ball on his head, beat the opposing goalkeeper and then headed his final effort over the crossbar because he'd had a row with his manager before the game.

Moreover, the old man swore he managed to see Len Hutton's 364 at The Oval by convincing the gate attendant that he was dying of some incurable disease and his last wish was to see Len before he took leave of this earth. I never swallowed that one until once at a football match where the gates were closed I witnessed him convince a gateman that he was a journalist and I was his runner. I was seven at the time, and it was the very first occasion I watched a football match from a press box.

Apart from being a fairy-story teller he was one of the best all-round sportsmen I have come across. He loved any game, and as soon as he took it up he played it well.

I never saw him play football, but I have been told that he did a fair imitation of Wilf Copping. As a cricketer he was a quick bowler with an action copied from his great hero, Harold Larwood.

He had a marvellous agility and a sure pair of hands near the bat, and as a batsman he was a genuine No 11 who often didn't know whether he'd play left- or right-handed until he got to the crease. Not that it made much difference.

Of all games he loved cricket the most. He judged everything and everyone by the game. The only time I ever saw him lost for words was when someone confessed they neither knew nor cared about cricket. Then he would shake his head, sadly baffled that a great part of his world – for cricket was surely that – could mean so little to any other sane human being. Once a friend and I took him to Headingley and sat him behind the bowler's arm and he never moved all day. We brought him pork pies and sandwiches and good Yorkshire beer, and he sat under his native sun watching Lillee bowl fast and he was the happiest man on our planet.

You always knew where my old man would be on any cricket ground: right behind the bowler's arm.

Moreover, if you ever lost him, or he lost himself – as he often did, being born without a sense of direction – you simply asked the whereabouts of the nearest cricket ground and there you would discover the old man sitting contentedly awaiting the arrival of his search party.

In his younger days his favourite holiday was a week at Scarbro' – which he reckoned had the best beach wicket in Britain – or Butlin's, not because he particularly cared for the idea of a holiday camp, but because of the sporting competitions. He used to enter the lot and normally came home with a couple of trophies for snooker or running or the mixed wheelbarrow race. He entered everything and anything and owed much of his success to his ability to talk an opponent to death. I once heard an irate tennis opponent say to him, 'Doesn't tha' ever shut thi' gob?'

'Only when other people are talking,' said my old man, with a disarming smile.

When he finished playing he took up coaching, first the local youngsters and latterly his three grandchildren. They, like me, are left-handed batsmen. Not because God made them so, but because the old man's theory was that not many players like bowling to left-handers. His other theory, based on a lifetime's experience, was that fast bowlers are crazy, so he determined to make at least one of my sons a slow bowler.

The consequence of this is that I once had the only eight-year-old googly bowler in the northern hemisphere. At ten he added the top-spinner to his repertoire and when he was twelve the old man's face was a picture as his protégé beat me with a googly and then had me plumb in front of the dustbin with one that hurried off the pitch and came straight through.

The old man's name was John William, and he hated John Willy. If anyone addressed him thus when he was playing in his prime, the red alert went up and the casualty ward at Barnsley Beckett Hospital could look forward to receiving visitors.

He's been dead for many years now, but I still think about him because he was a special man and I was lucky to know him. He was a Yorkshireman, a miner, a humorist and a fast bowler. Not a bad combination.

I only hope they play cricket in heaven. If they don't he'll ask for a transfer.

This book is a tender tribute to a wonderful man, an attempt to understand the grip of grief and the emotional minefield that is the relationship between a father and a son, and to see how much was passed on to me by him and what still lives within me. It is at its heart a love letter from me and every part of my family lucky enough to know my father, John William Parkinson.

It is, however, a book that has also had a long gestation period, mainly because of my resistance to it. It is one that my friend and long-time publisher, Roddy Bloomfield, has had in mind ever since he began compiling the pieces that I wrote for the *Sunday Times* and other publications into books on cricket, football and sport in general and discovered that, alongside 'Skinner' Normanton, 'Muscle' Eadie and other sporting luminaries of my youth, the figure that appeared most prominently in my pen portraits of sport in a northern mining village and the role it played in my childhood was my father.

Roddy's appetite for a book that concentrates upon this enormous influence on my life was increased by the publication of my autobiography, *Parky*, in 2008. He has been politely pushing the issue ever since, whilst I have been politely diverting his attention with offerings on Muhammad Ali and George Best, as well as some fulsome pitching of other ideas for books, such as the history of the Grimethorpe Colliery Band, a celebration of the hitherto little-known sport of South Yorkshire competitive clog dancing and a cookery book entitled *Parky's 100 Recipes with Forced Rhubarb*.

Undeterred, Roddy has kept up the pressure, but being a man of impeccable manners, his insistence makes me feel like a recalcitrant sinner being pursued by a softly spoken, bookish Monsignor. However, there is a serious reason why I've only got around to writing this now and that's because I felt that in the pieces I mentioned above I had told my father's story, or at least in the way I wanted to remember it, and in so doing made clear my love for him and the influence he has had on me. But then I agreed to appear on Piers Morgan's talk show and the book was finally born.

CHAPTER 1

LIFE STORIES

'There is a type of snobbish, pompous journalist who thinks
that the only news that has any validity is war, famine,
pestilence or politics. I don't come from that school.'

Piers Morgan

Preparing the wicket for beach cricket. Scarborough, 1938.

BEFORE PIERS MORGAN'S DESIRE TO hold our largely ineffectual and incompetent political masters' 'feet to the fire' for the handling of the pandemic had elevated him to a renewed position of eminence and respect among fellow journalists, I was a somewhat lone voice in my appreciation of his talent. He is certainly a divisive, controversial figure, with an ego that at times can make him capable of moments of crass showboating, but his command of the live television environment, his intelligence and breadth of interests and his journalistic instincts make him a compelling performer. I was not prepared, however, for him to be the most unlikely inspiration for this book.

I had for a number of years declined his many invitations to appear on his show *Life Stories*. I'd always had a slight problem with the format, which mixes a traditional 'life and times' talk show with elements of *This is Your Life*, and I'm also uncomfortable with what seems to be the entire purpose of the show, which is to guarantee the spectacle of lachrymose celebrities. However, having now personally endured the three-hour-plus recording time, part of me suspects that for some guests the tears are caused not by a painful memory but by the dawning realisation that they may not see their homes again before the World's End.

Then a couple of years ago Piers kindly gave up his time to do an interview with me in aid of the Lord's Taverners, of which I was then president, and we agreed as a quid pro quo that I would appear on *Life Stories*. I found Piers to be a combative, engaging interviewee and we covered a range of subjects, from sport to the price of fame and his then close relationship with President Trump, whilst also revealing that he must have a strong death wish, given his decision to become human target practice for the Australian fast bowler Brett Lee in the nets of Melbourne Cricket Ground – not to mention his choice to use his position as host of his own CNN show in America to stand up to the NRA gun lobbyists, who have members that prefer to settle arguments with an assault rifle rather than an on-air debate.

Piers was a great addition to the Taverners event, which raised thousands to enable underprivileged and disabled kids access to cricket, that most glorious of games. And so it came to pass that I found myself sitting in an Elstree recording studio opposite the Grand Inquisitor Piers Morgan.

I've been a journalist all my working life and I feel I know every trick of the trade and therefore as an interviewee I'm confident I know how to avoid the inconvenient question. So, despite being advised by those close to me that the sole purpose of the show would be to delve into potentially painful areas of my life, in an attempt to elicit the Holy Grail of a celebrity sob, I was fairly certain that I could avoid that particular fate. Knowing also that he likes a challenge, I had even told Piers before the interview that there was no way he was going to make me cry.

The fact is, I've had a charmed life: a largely untroubled upbringing, a strong and enduring marriage, sons who still talk to me and a career that for the most part has been fulfilling and lucrative. The only really difficult times I have had were dealing with the death of my father and the overwhelming grief that threatened to derail me, plus my brief sojourn into the sad backwater of a drink problem. But I have openly talked and written about both, explaining that they were not wholly but definitely interlinked, and moreover they happened over thirty years ago, so I had no reason to suspect that I would become another entry in Piers Morgan's Hall of Fame sponsored by Kleenex (other brands are available). How wrong I was. When he asked me about losing my father I didn't just cry, I sobbed. I was taken completely by surprise.

In the aftermath of the show I tried to rationalise why it had happened. Why did this particular interview open up a door to my feelings about my father that had been kept, to anyone outside the family and close friends, maybe not fully shut but at least only partly ajar? Looking back now, I think the reason may lie in the fact that I was not fully prepared for how different *Life Stories* would be from any other televised interview I had done before. It was an interesting but unsettling experience, because the style was so foreign to me.

My aim as an interviewer was always to establish a 'relationship' and rapport with, a couple of exceptions aside, a person who is basically a stranger in even stranger surroundings. I achieved that, I believe, by being 'reactive' in my style of interviewing, in the sense that I always prepared as well and as diligently as I could, shaping the interview into an editorially linked and justified series of questions. I went into each encounter confident of my subject, which gave me licence to listen carefully to the answers and judge the mood and demeanour of the guest in order to be ready to, as it were, go 'off script'.

The result was that if, as often happened, my initial questions elicited an answer to a question I was planning to ask later in the interview, or if a general response in either body language or tone in the interviewee indicated that access to their story down that particular avenue was going to be difficult, I could seek an alternative, even if perhaps it wasn't exactly the interview I had in mind. It's a style that suited my personality, and I believe some of my very best interviews have been when I have only asked perhaps one or two of my prepared questions and it has then developed into a natural free-flowing conversation.

The other thing I always insisted on was that the programme should be done as if 'live'. If it overran by too much – anything over twenty minutes – to me it was a bad sign in that it indicated I had felt the need to go 'fishing' beyond the scope of the prepared interview because I was unsure of the quality of what we had already recorded. In a sense, I produced the interview as I conducted it, wary of leaving too much to be done in the edit, which always, to my mind, resulted in a stilted, unnatural end product.

There are exceptions, of course. In their prime, Billy Connolly, Peter Ustinov, David Attenborough and the like could and should, for the benefit of the common weal, have been interviewed nightly for at least an hour until they ran out of things to say, or more likely the interviewer reached retirement age. But most interviewers should heed the maxim of the late Conservative politician Lord Mancroft, whose advice, although he was specifically talking about making a speech, can easily be applied to the arena of the interview: 'A speech is like a love affair – any fool can start one, but to end it requires considerable skill.'

Piers is no fool, but he is a very different beast to me. He approaches an interview for *Life Stories* as if it is a profile piece for a magazine, in that there is seemingly no time limit to the interview and the shape will be decided after he has reviewed all the footage. The effect on the interviewee is that you leave with little sense of how it went except that you may have said too much or been too unguarded, and slightly concerned about how the content will be shaped once it disappears into the edit suite. It's as if you've been gently turned over by a Savile Row-suited mugger.

He's a very bright man, a good interviewer, but it quickly becomes clear he is not much interested in a free-flowing, mutually led conversation. He has decided what he wants you to talk about and *when* he wants you to talk about it. I think I am a very easy interviewee, in that I know how difficult it can be if the participant is unwilling, and therefore I try to frame my answers in a way that leads the interviewer to the most interesting parts of my life as quickly as possible, although it is also true that, like most of us who are in the public eye, I do tend to fall back on the tried-and-tested anecdotes, some of which admittedly through overexposure have begun to lose some of their lustre. I tried this approach early on with Piers but he was having none of it. In *Life Stories* you are very much a subject in the Court of King Piers, and in his iron grip no amount of obfuscation or verbal wriggling on your part will throw him off the scent.

The interview is divided into structured sections in which certain aspects of your life are picked over in painstaking detail until he is satisfied, and no deviation from or abbreviation of this section is allowed. He also gives a masterclass in emotional manipulation as he constantly prevents you from falling back into your protective routine of remembrance by asking you to think afresh about the events in your life and to express your feelings about them, reassuring you that it is 'only human' to have feelings. He then dripfeeds into the interview filmed inserts of contributions from dear friends and beloved family members, often as a punctuation mark to signify the beginning of a new section but also as a way to augment the feeling that you are being slowly led to a crescendo lurking somewhere in the third hour of the programme. And bang on cue, as we entered the third hour of the interview, Piers asked me about the two aspects of my life that, as I have said, have caused the most difficulty.

The first rapier thrust, concerning my drinking, was parried easily enough. I have been very open about my drink problem, which began to take hold at around the time the first run of *Parkinson* was coming to a close. I have been asked many times in interviews about why and how, as the great Sir Les Patterson put it, I 'gave the grog a nudge', so I had no problem talking again about what I thought were the causes, how bad it got and the role that my wife Mary played in getting me by the short and curlies and pulling me back onto the right track. As with many addictions, the causes are complicated and myriad, a mixture of genetic and environmental, but it was definitely the case that one contributing factor was the death of my father. Cue the next *En garde*. Again, I was unconcerned and perfectly happy to talk about this. I believed that while I had perhaps not fully come to terms with it – let's face it, who does – I had packed it safely away in the jumbled attic of my memories to ensure I was sufficiently insulated against it.

To be honest, I don't know what happened. I was certainly totally unprepared for the violence of my reaction. Perhaps it was what had gone before: remembering events in a fresh way; the constant refrain of not being ashamed of feelings; the heartfelt and moving filmed inserts, particularly the one featuring my eldest boy, Andrew, being visibly moved when he was talking about his grandfather. Or perhaps it was the growing feeling that I might need to spend a night in the local Travelodge (not that there is anything wrong with that, except I don't like the pillows) if the interview wasn't brought to an end soon.

All that undoubtedly prepared the ground, but the tipping point was the simple yet skilful question Piers asked. He didn't deal in generalities but asked me specifically to recall feelings that come to mind when I think about the day my father died and, like Banquo at the feast, into my head sprang a terrible image that had lurked in the shadows for so long.

We had brought my father home to die and when he passed away, I couldn't cope with the organisation of the removal of the body to the funeral home. It meant that I was unprepared for the sight of my beloved dad being removed by two strangers in what amounted to a large zip-up plastic bag. It was this image that for some reason came into my mind when Piers asked the question.

As is true of most men of my generation, crying does not come easily, and in my book crying in public on a national television show is a definite no-no. But the tears came and when they did it was difficult to stop them. I was overwhelmed by a whole raft of unexpected emotions. Thinking back, I now know what is meant by that tired old cliché of your life flashing before your eyes.

For me it was not a highlights reel of my life but a jumble of emotions that came cascading from God knows what hiding place. There was grief certainly, and a sense of loss, but also regret and shame, mixed with a sense of wonder that such a man had been my dad. To rationalise, process and express all these feelings at that moment was impossible. I was paralysed. Pinned like a rare butterfly.

To his credit, Piers, with suitable care and no little skill, ensured the moment didn't become too uncomfortable for me, the studio audience or the viewer by empathising and by asking me to try to explain why I still felt my father's loss so strongly. I simply answered that it was because he was a much better man than I was. Pick the bones out of that, Sigmund Freud.

*　　*　　*

John William Parkinson, beloved father, with
Freda Rose Parkinson, a mettlesome woman.

My son Mike was at the recording and we met afterwards to talk about what had occurred. He was as shocked as I was that a man who had died more than forty years ago could still affect me in that way. As we mulled this over and also considered the way Andrew had spoken so movingly about his grandfather, an idea began to form. We looked at each other and both said perhaps Roddy is right, there is a book there, but maybe not in the way he envisaged it.

The book that has emerged is much more than simply a collection of reminiscences, many of which are contained in some of the better articles I wrote about my father – though we will still revisit these as they remain enlightening, stand the test of time and still capture the sense of my relationship with him and the nature of the man. They recall his sporting obsessions, his sense of humour and his lifelong determination to produce, from either his son or three grandsons, a cricketer worthy of playing for his beloved Yorkshire. (In that sense we are all a huge disappointment to him.)

But in addition, and for the first time, the book also attempts to explore where my father came from and what shaped him in life before I was even a twinkling in his eye. On top of that it's the story of my dad, John William Parkinson, told from my son Mike's perspective and it reveals how, as a grandfather and father-in-law, he touched and transformed every member of the family. Which is why it is written in relay form, with Mike and me taking turns to move the story forward. As a consequence, the book contains two distinctive but complementary viewpoints which get to the heart of this fascinating family story but also prove that, in writing ability at least, the apple has not fallen far from the tree. We have also delved into the treasure trove of the *Parkinson* archive to learn more about the often fraught and complicated relationship between fathers and sons.

'Like father, like son.' It's a tired old axiom and one that is often used as a mild form of insult to the son, an aside accompanied by a knowing smile, for behaviour that recalls unwelcome memories of his father's frailties. For this book, it is neither a rebuke nor a statement but a question to which we will look for an answer. But given what I already know about my father's life before I was born, it is one that should have a very large and bold question mark after it.

CHAPTER 2

IT'S GRIM UP NORTH

'Those who decry mining are ignorant of history. If they knew anything . . . they would know that all business, all industry and all human progress depend on mines.'

William Sulzer, Governor of New York, 1938

The Rock Cinema: 'the focal point of my life'.

I WAS BORN EIGHTY-FIVE YEARS AGO in a mining village called Cudworth and whenever anyone asks me to tell them what my childhood was like I suggest they read an article I wrote that featured in *Parkinson's Lore*. Memories of days past and in particular your childhood are not something that should be relied upon too readily. They are liable to be dipped in sepia-tinted tears and perfumed with the aroma of freshly baked bread, accompanied by the purring of a marmalade cat on the hearth and the sound of Mother's lullabies. But scrape away the romantic tone and poetic licence of this piece and what remains is an accurate reflection of the safe, comfortable childhood I lived and the one my parents built for me.

I was born in a council house in the Yorkshire mining village of Cudworth on a housing estate nicknamed 'Debtors' Retreat', where the rent collectors walked in pairs. As a kid growing up there it helped if you could either fight or run. I was a runner.

I liked the place. It was ragged-arsed, snotty-nosed and ugly, but it was never boring. It had four or five Nonconformist chapels, six or seven boozers and one cinema which became the focal point of my life. It was called The Rock for reasons which had something to do with the seats, and it was here that I fell in love with Joan Leslie and Cyd Charisse, who were confections of the Dream Factory, and Pat Heaton and Mavis Lodge, who were not, but whom I never got to sit with on the back row.

I spent the greater part of my childhood in the cinema. I went every Sunday, Monday, Wednesday and Friday, which was when they changed the programmes. If I didn't turn up they used to send someone down to our house to find out what was wrong. In what passed for the cultural society of Cudworth, going to the pictures was better than wasting your money at the boozer – but not as uplifting as going to chapel and listening to the *Messiah*.

Every one of the chapels used to produce its version of the *Messiah* each year and it seemed to me that the work was in production for ten months out of the twelve in

our village. I had a friend whose family were keen
chapel-goers and *Messiah* addicts and, once a year, I'd be
scrubbed until I glowed, polished till I shone like a
guardsman's toecap and sent to my mate's house.
There we would sit on horsehair chairs draped with
antimacassars in the best room, which was only used
on *Messiah* days or when someone died.

I can smell the musty scent of that room even now. I
can see the twilight filtering through lace curtains that
were only ever moved an inch to see who was passing by.
We would gather in the room to sip elderberry wine –
which was the nearest my mate's parents ever got to a
rave-up. Then we would be off to the chapel to sit on
spine-breaking benches while the local lads in the choir
belted out the words with real vigour, without moving a
strand of their concreted hair; and the visiting soloists,
with quivering Adam's apples and jellied bosoms, won a
bonus point from the Almighty and a few quid in the
back pocket as well.

Like all mining communities it was enclosed and
self-sufficient. Visitors were welcome but likely to be
regarded with friendly curiosity rather than real
warmth. The cockney evacuees who came to our
village were not treated as waifs but strangers from

31

another planet. They could have been Martians for all we knew.

The first real-life American I ever saw was a soldier who was going out with one of the local girls. He looked like an extra from *Hollywood Canteen* or some such movie and I followed him and his girlfriend wherever they went with eyes stuck out like chapel hat-pegs. I was convinced he lived at The Rock with John Wayne.

It was a village where nothing was secret, where any private family crisis very soon became common knowledge. This meant, in the main, a caring community, but it could also be a cruel one.

I remember a girl, blonde and attractive, who became pregnant without first bothering to get married. I was standing at a bus-stop one day and she passed by, carrying her sin in front of her. 'She ought to have it sewn up,' said a woman in the queue, loud enough for the girl to hear. Although, at the time, I wasn't exactly sure of what she meant, I was in no doubt about the sentiment.

Yet this was also a village where you didn't need to lock your back door, where real tragedy – like sudden bereavement – was coddled and anaesthetised by genuine concern; where no child would ever be an orphan.

It was also a place of ritual where the horrid hours spent underground getting coal were countered with leisure activities that were seriously worked at. There was nothing dilettante about the allotment men, pigeon fanciers, cricketers, whippet breeders, part-time singers and snooker players.

Recreation was the antidote to a lifetime working down the mine and therefore something to be taken seriously. You didn't play cricket for fun, nor grow parsnips only to eat. These activities were taken up to prove that you were the *best* cricketer in Cudworth or that you could grow the *biggest* parsnip. And if you didn't shape up, that was all the more reason to work much harder at your hobby.

Boozing, too, was an antidote and a ritual. If I carry one lasting memory of life in a Yorkshire pit village it is of the moment before the pubs opened on Sunday lunchtime.

Ten minutes before noon the clients would congregate in little, silent groups a fair distance from the closed doors. With thirty seconds to opening time, and without anyone looking at a watch, they would move with unhurried tread towards the pub. As they arrived at the door it would open, as if by magic. If it didn't, it was the landlord who had got it wrong and never the lads. What is more, he would likely need a new door.

Having been around a bit since I left there, I can't think of another place I would rather have grown up in. There are prettier places, no doubt, and healthier, too. But none where you felt that body-warmth, that sense of being an ordinary, vulnerable human both taking from and giving to those around you. That is not a nostalgic statement, rather a definition of my taproots.

Now, it has always been a particular bugbear of mine that whenever you mention that you come from a mining village, there is a tendency for the listener to adopt a sympathetic pose, as if it is a cross you have had to bear all your life and your talent was a gift because it allowed you to escape the grimy, suffocating, desperate confines of your slag-heaped prison. This is not and has never been the case – well, certainly not for me.

There were areas of deprivation and desperation, of course. Even for those in work, real poverty, by which I mean destitution, not the modern incarnation of having to choose between Sky TV or a pack of fags, was only an accident or a feckless attitude to life away. There were families mired in dysfunction and the social problems that come with that. But for the majority, and for the people that I lived in close proximity to, the picture I represent was as real and as nurturing as I report it. And I'm not alone in remembering it that way.

I am the patron of a community magazine called *Chewin' the Cud* which is run by a group of volunteers who make it their mission to be a repository of memories of my hometown of Cudworth. Looking back over past issues, it is clear how much freedom and fun we had as children. The contributors fondly recall the times they took over the streets mob-handed and filled the evening air with the shrieks, shouts and laughter that accompanied cricket, football and other more imaginative games like 'run sheep run', in which more than fifty children would separate into groups of 'sheep' and 'wolves' and go howling and careering through the streets. There was no traffic, the streets were empty, no televisual or digital temptation, and we had safety in numbers and a local bobby to prevent undue rioting.

As the stories reveal, Cudworth itself was a well-provided, self-contained community with a Co-op, a newsagents, a hardware store and, that staple of Yorkshire mining villages, a fish and chip shop, with a doctor and a dentist's clinic a mile away. Although the Grimethorpe pithead dominated the immediate skyline, our playgrounds were not, as the

Cudworth: 'a definition of my taproots'.

accepted wisdom of the time would have it, the slag heaps, for alongside the streets there were the fields and meadows of the surrounding countryside, including Storrs Mill Wood, a source of bluebells in the spring and blackberries in the autumn. Yet this preconceived notion of the bleakness of a mining childhood and upbringing remains an enduring and unwelcome myth.

Even today, when I talk about my birthplace during the live shows that I do around the country with my son Mike, people still find it difficult to believe that I and my friends didn't live and play in the forbidding shadow of some 'dark Satanic mill' belching fire and brimstone. They seem surprised when I talk fondly about it and make it clear that in general, despite growing up in the grim monochrome world of the 1950s, the life of a child in Cudworth was not something to elicit dewy-eyed sympathy. I have had to disabuse people of this idea all my life, including, in a slightly bizarre fashion, a friend, colleague and someone as bright as the late Russell Harty.

A Lancastrian by birth, Russell sensibly crossed the Pennines to first teach English at a school in Giggleswick and then to make his home there, once television became his career and his true calling. Whilst I was first hosting *Parkinson*, he ploughed his own particular furrow in the interview game on BBC2 and, given our contrasting styles, we sat comfortably alongside each other. In his later career he hosted a series of travelogues and the one he cut his teeth with was a grand tour of Yorkshire, for which he chose me as one of his travelling companions. After many pleasant hours of Russell filming luscious views of the Dales and talking to characters residing in chocolate-box cottages in equally picturesque villages I found myself, in the company of Russell, walking up the side of a slag heap near Grimethorpe pit and I realised that the real reason I was involved was to act as the grit in the eye of this sumptuous programme.

Our journey was captured in long shot with no sound and presumably would be accompanied by the strains of the Grimethorpe Colliery Band and a hushed-toned voice-over lamenting my deprived childhood. I was not dressed for the occasion and the wind whipping off the Pennines was in danger of giving my extremities frostbite, whilst the slag heap was making mincemeat of a nice pair of Italian loafers. Not being miked up for sound, I decided to ask Russell in no uncertain terms what we were doing. He said he thought it would be informative for the viewer to see me revisit the playground of my youth. In equally robust terms, I suggested he was talking out of his fundament and we began our descent.

If you still don't believe me, let me quote you something written by that firebrand of the socialist chattering class George Orwell, whose overriding concern and idea of fun was to write books and articles fomenting a class war by sticking it to the ruling class and the way their attitudes and politics have for the working class meant a life akin to 'a boot stamping on a human face – for ever'. In his book *The Road to Wigan Pier*, first published in 1937, he undertook his own grand tour of the industrial north in order to report on living and working conditions. It is for the most part a bleak and unsparing read, but although he found much to assuage the social conscience of his followers warming their toes by the fires of their Bloomsbury living rooms, he was forced to concede that where, as I have described, the households were inhabited by decent, hard-working people, things were not 'arf bad'.

In a working-class home – I am not thinking at the moment of the unemployed, but of comparatively pros- perous homes – you breathe a warm, decent, deeply human atmosphere which it is not so easy to find else- where. I should say that a manual worker, if he is in steady work and drawing good wages – an 'if' which gets bigger and bigger – has a better chance of being happy than an 'educated' man. His home life seems to fall more naturally into a sane and comely shape. I have often been struck by the peculiar easy completeness, the perfect symmetry as it were, of a working-class interior at its best. Especially on winter evenings after tea, when the fire glows in the open range and dances mirrored in the steel fender, when Father, in shirt-sleeves, sits in the rocking chair at one side of the fire reading the racing finals, and Mother sits on the other with her sewing, and the children are happy with a pennorth of mint humbugs, and the dog lolls roasting himself on the rag mat – it is a good place to be in.

Now, George Orwell and I are not natural literary bedfellows. He wasn't a cricket fan, though he did reveal one shared love when he wrote a lovely fictional depiction of an idyllic English pub called 'The Moon under Water', but, and I'm not one to blow my own trumpet, it is clear that although I generally write better gags than him, we can also agree, surprisingly given his political sensibilities, that the working class were and are more than capable of lifting themselves above what they did for a living or their environment and aspiring to a better life for them and their children without the need for pointless schemes and condescending articles and speeches by people far removed from their life and experiences. The last thing the working class need, as the 2019 election so resoundingly proved, is patronising sympathy.

The real opium of the people is the provision of conditions that offer equality of opportunity. Give them that and they'll replace their terraces with palaces. It was my mother who created these conditions at home. She approached the task as assiduously as she did driving me to make the best of my talents. Indeed, her love for both of the men in her life was tinged with a desire for us to make the most of what we had: for me to achieve what she believed I should with the talent for writing that was evident from an early age, and for my father to go against his nature and be ambitious in order to ensure that we never had to scrimp and save and, despite the odd occasion when we had to hide from the aforementioned rent collectors, she was determined that it was never the Parkinsons who were the subject of the sympathetic head-shaking gossip of the village.

My mother was not a native of South Yorkshire. She had been born in Oxford, but after her father had been killed in the Great War her mother remarried, to a Yorkshireman, and the family relocated to Cudworth. I always believe that her childhood spent living maybe not in the shadows of the dreaming spires but somewhere fundamentally different to the Yorkshire mining village she fetched up in by pure chance goes some way to explain why I have written in the past about how she was a thwarted and frustrated person, unhappy with her lot in life, which was also not helped by the fact she was a woman born with a brain at a time when

Me and Mum: 'She averaged over 20 on
Scarborough beach and was a useful
donkey-drop bowler.'

that was not someone recognised as existing. She could never forget the pain of the injustice that her schooling was cut short so she could go to work to help pay for her brother Tom to go to Oxford University; could never get over the fact that the family also placed itself in a debt they had no chance of paying off, just so Tom and not her could go on to further education.

She wanted a Cotswold village and marriage to a local doctor, not a mining village and a Yorkshire miner, no matter how much she deeply loved my father and he her, with an almost canine devotion that lasted all their married life. My wife Mary remembers witnessing a particularly touching scene of matrimonial harmony: they were sitting together in later life and while my mum knitted, my father carefully peeled pieces of fruit for her, just so she wouldn't get her hands sticky and damage her handiwork. But despite this love match, she always considered herself an outsider and in many ways felt confined by the pit village, whereas my father was a Yorkshireman in outlook and interests to his very core – a fact my mother discovered on the very first day they were married, as I recalled in an article I wrote for the *Sunday Times*:

My mother had not realised when she married my father that she was taking on the Yorkshire County Cricket Club as well.

The realisation first dawned on her honeymoon, which Father persuaded her to take in London. The trip from Barnsley to London in those days was a glamorous one and my mother was overjoyed at his thoughtfulness.

43

What she didn't realise was that Yorkshire were playing Middlesex at Lord's and she spent three days behind the bowler's arm while her husband sat, as he always did at any cricket match, with a huge smile on his face, as if he was the happiest man alive.

By the time I had arrived upon Yorkshire soil and was able to stand up and hold a cricket bat, my mother had become a fair all-rounder. She averaged over 20 on Scarborough beach and was a useful donkey-drop bowler. Her sister, Auntie Madge, was our wicketkeeper and there have been few better standing up using a coat. They were both coached by my father, who believed anyone born in Yorkshire, man or woman, had a duty to play cricket.

We played cricket all the time. When I look back at my youth it was one long cricket match interrupted now and then by totally unnecessary matters like learning algebra or conjugating Latin verbs.

And after I arrived the stork never revisited our house in Cudworth and whether by accident or design – it wasn't the sort of thing you asked your parents then – my status as an only child economically and domestically elevated us above households full to the brim with offspring. As my old sparring partner George Orwell noted, the best-appointed households in the industrial north were the ones with only one or two children, because the money earned by the miner went further. In the days before utility rooms and white goods, the keeping clean and orderly of a household inhabited by a large brood and a man who returned every day from work filthy and starving was a task that could turn a pretty young maid into a broken-down drudge. This was not to be the fate of my mother or her family.

The breadwinner, my father, was a miner from the age of fourteen. He worked in conditions unimaginable to the average man or woman and he did it without complaint until ill health forced him to retire in his early sixties. When I think about my father, there is no word in the English language that captures what he endured in order to give me and my mother a comfortable home life. He gave us the chance to indulge our shared liking of losing ourselves in books and being entranced by Hollywood movie stars, as well as a new cricket bat for me every season and a pair of shiny boots of the type worn by my hero Danny Blanchflower. Both of us have a lot to thank him for.

Coal mining is now a defunct industry, its product rightly demonised, with its communities disbanded, its workforce forgotten and discarded. Yet we owe so much that we take for granted in our everyday lives to decades of sweat and toil by men like my father underground. It was the industry that from the mid- to late-nineteenth century onwards produced the material that literally fired the Industrial Revolution and catapulted Britain and the world into the modern mechanised age. Think of that next time you turn on the light, boil an egg or shop on Amazon.

Moreover, my father worked at Grimethorpe pit, part of the Barnsley Seam of the South Yorkshire Coalfield which, as I always suspected as a child, was of the greatest importance of all the seams in the South Yorkshire area. Indeed, if I am able to further indulge myself for a moment, I would like to point out that alongside the fact that Yorkshire is the largest county, with more acres than words in the Bible, and that 'those feet' most likely walked upon Ilkley Moor and not Glastonbury Tor, it is a source of additional pride to discover that we also had, in terms of quality and quantity, the richest deposits of coal in the whole of the country, accounting for more than 15 per cent of national output at its height.

Yorkshire and its miners played a significant part in the industry that transformed the world we live in. We should all be grateful that men like my father did a dirty and dangerous job so we could go about our everyday lives in a manner to which we have become accustomed without a second thought as to how it came to be. So also think on that when you are lucky enough to see the Yorkshire and England captain Joe Root score a century in a floodlit test.

The location and the name of the pit where my father worked is about the limit of my knowledge of what the life of an average miner was like. So when we set out to chart the history of my father's early life and his time as a miner we employed a genealogist called Susan Collins. She diligently chipped away at her chosen coalface of birth and death certificates, employment records and local newspapers but, in her words, came up 'disappointed and frustrated but not surprised' because, as she lamented when handing over the research, the working lives of miners only warrant a mention in official documentation when they are either severely injured or killed. My father was, to my eyes, a great man but he was not a 'Great Man' worthy of a detailed life story used as a lesson to others, but a mere cog in an uncaring and exploitative industrial machine that spat him out ill and diminished at the end of his usefulness to it.

With this gaping hole in our knowledge revealed, it was therefore necessary for my son Mike to return to his roots as a history undergraduate and attempt to build a possible picture of my father's life underground from collections of first-hand accounts of miners and other sources.

It was for him a labour of love, and I was impressed by the way he immersed himself in his subject. I would often find him in the office we share with all the blinds closed and him working by the light of a solitary Davy safety lamp. He adopted a canary and called it John William. He went online and purchased a coal shovel once used by a miner in Grimethorpe pit and would in moments of reflection be found reverentially stroking it, and on many occasions we had to indulge him when he insisted on demonstrating the technique needed to extract coal whilst employing the pillar-and-stall method. Ex-miners reading this book will know of what I speak.

What follows is the result of Mike attempting to fill in the details of an incomplete picture. It is only an approximation of what my dad, his grandad, did for a living but it should give you an idea of what he endured. It is a shocking and revealing account of human exploitation on an industrial scale. I'll leave you in Mike's capable hands.

CHAPTER 3

OLD KING COAL

Long is the way
And hard, that out of Hell leads up to light.

John Milton, *Paradise Lost*

Grimethorpe Colliery: the workplace of my grandfather
from the age of fourteen.

ONE OF THE THINGS THAT most intrigued me about my grandfather was the fact that he was a miner. It was a job that shaped and defined him as a man and ultimately prematurely curtailed his life but about which my understanding only, excuse the pun, scratched the surface. However, on researching the industry I was quite unprepared to discover just how horrific the job actually was and for the most part how appallingly miners of my grandfather's generation were treated. For that reason what follows is part history, part polemic.

My grandfather's life was mapped out for him from the day he was born, on 4 December 1903, in Shafton, a pit village in the shadow of Grimethorpe Colliery. He was the third child of Samuel Parkinson and Florence Kate Parkinson (née Sawyer). His father was described as a 'colliery repairman dataller': not a permanent employee but a day man paid for work on the basis of when he was required. He would most likely have been called on to clear and repair underground roadways after rock falls and replace broken or defective pit props. Money was therefore unpredictable and tight, and in the era when mines were owned by individuals generally unconcerned with the lives of their employees, my grandfather would almost certainly have grown up in overcrowded, insanitary housing.

When the Sankey Commission was set up in 1919, it was the first time in the long history of the industry that a fully rounded investigation into working and living conditions had been undertaken. It condemned those of the average mining family as 'a reproach to civilisation'. One of the authors of the report, Sidney Webb, asked the question 'Why do twice as many babies die in a miner's cottage as in a middle-class home?', knowing that it was the dirt and discomfort of their homes and the stress placed on miners' wives that was the cause.

And so it was that John William Parkinson's childhood was a flurry of births and deaths of siblings. In 1911, when he was seven, he was living with his five brothers and sisters, aged between ten and five months, in a five-room house in High Street, Shafton. Twins arrived in 1913, but between 1911 and 1916, three of these children died from a variety of childhood ailments, including that scourge of the young, measles. What they would have done for a vaccine then.

His parents went on to have two more children, with the last arriving when Florence was forty-two. On learning this, my dad, apart from being impressed at the physical fortitude of his grandmother, was more amazed that the small, stone-deaf, lugubrious, unassuming Grandad Sammy that he knew had such vim in him! I did point out that it rains a lot in Yorkshire.

In 1894, the Mitchell Main Colliery Company held a cere-mony for the 'turning of the first sod' for the new Grimethorpe Colliery, hosted by the managing director, Mr Joseph Mitchell of Bolton Hall. Following speeches in which, and I kid you not, regret was expressed that the new mine would ruin the best part of the Badsworth hunt country, there commenced a fine lunch accompanied by even finer wine, topped off with cigars and liqueurs. All to mark the sinking of a hole nearly 1000 metres deep that would be the appall-ing workplace of men and children, most of whom had to work there whether they wanted to or not. They should have marked the occasion with a minute's silence, or perhaps more pertinently they should have, as we did for front-line

53

health workers doing a difficult job few of us could do but all of us relied on, joined in a communal and fulsome round of applause.

At the age of fourteen my grandfather achieved the 'leaving standard' at the local school of basic literacy and numeracy and was therefore able to leave and go to work in the only place that a young man born in Shafton could. He had no choice: the family had hungry mouths to feed. John William began work at Grimethorpe in 1917, the same year that the famous Grimethorpe Colliery Band was formed. Who'd have thought, two of the great loves of my dad's life, John William and brass band music, would emerge at the same time from the same hole in the ground in South Yorkshire.

On his first day he would have walked the three miles from his home to arrive at the pit by 5.30 in the morning shod in either clogs or, if he was lucky, new or hand-me-down pit boots, with his snap tin and flask of water or cold tea in hand. It would be easy to smile and scoff at an image that seems almost an amalgamation of the Hovis bread TV advert and Monty Python's 'Four Yorkshiremen' sketch but this was the reality for my grandfather and there was nothing amusing or romantic about what faced him and his classmates. They would not have had an inkling of what awaited them when they first stepped into what would be their workplace for the rest of their productive lives.

I can't imagine what they must have been feeling. I know I would have been terrified, just as my dad was when, as a child, he made his one and only visit to his father's workplace. My grandfather took my dad down the mine simply to disabuse him of any idea he might have had that mining was a job prospect for him. It's a story my dad has told so many times that it has lost some of its power, but it was vividly brought back to life for him and for me when, on a research trip up north, we visited the wonderful National Coal Mining Museum, built on the site of the old Caphouse Colliery in Overton near Wakefield. Alongside an extensive research library and archive, it boasts a fascinating museum that appeals to old and young, ex-miners and civilians alike, plus an underground tour of the now-defunct mine, which has been made accessible and safe to us surface-dwellers.

From the moment we stepped into the 'cage', which descended at a more sedate pace than the fairground-ride speed with which they hurtled down in my grandfather's day, particularly if a 'newbie' was on board, I immediately began to feel a growing sense of claustrophobic unease, and

I know my dad was being transported back to that day when he and his father were crammed in with thirty-odd men, heading to what seemed like Hell.

At the bottom of Caphouse Colliery it's the closest they could make it to a Walt Disney-theme-park imagining of a mine. The walls have been whitewashed, the ground is level, the air cool and clean, the only noises the occasional excited shrieks or careless laughter of children – in complete contrast to the day when my dad, in the company of my grandfather,

The descent to Hell.

stepped from the cage and was immediately assailed by a cacophony of men, machines and the groaning, shifting rocks and protesting coal seams, all baking in a fetid soup of overheated, stinking air that must have overwhelmed the senses and made my dad want to turn and run for the green hills. No wonder he decided against following his father down there, and thank God my grandfather never wanted him near the place.

The guided tour was conducted by an ex-collier with the bravado and bluff gallows humour typical of anyone who has had to endure such working conditions. It's a coping mechanism, a protective carapace to shield them from the reality of their daily working life, a defence against the human instinct to think too deeply about their lot. (John Milton, that Poet Laureate of all subterranean toilers, put it more eloquently when he wrote, 'The mind is its own place, and in itself can make a heaven of hell, a hell of heaven.') Everything about our guide was broad, from his accent to his shoulders and his smile. With passion, humour and hard-earned knowledge, he took us through the history of how men, women and children have hewed coal from the earth, from way before a young Geoffrey Boycott was practising his forward defensive in his bedroom mirror. It was informative and entertaining but also a salutary lesson in man's inhumanity to man and a damning indictment of what the class system can do to the dispossessed.

Accompanying us on this trip was my son Felix, a lovely, gangly, happy-go-lucky sixteen-year-old who, at over 6 ft 2 in, is a good six inches taller than his great grandfather, whom he never met, though he shares his love of cricket and in particular, I'm pleased to say, of the five-day variety. We came to a part of the mine which had been kept, give or take a lick of whitewash, as it would have been when the mine was still working. Suddenly we were faced with a low corridor of rock held up by props which the miners would have had to negotiate bent double. This one was only a few metres in length but our guide advised us that miners would often have to travel for a mile or so in even more cramped conditions than that to get to their place of work. It was, even in this sanitised, user-friendly form, both claustrophobic and forbidding.

There was an alternative route which avoided the strong possibility of having to spend the next week at a chiropractor. My dad and I sensibly took this but Felix, in that way of all young men when in the company of older male relatives, decided to display his burgeoning masculinity by taking on this test of suppleness. As he made his way towards the coalface, bent over, he turned and grinned triumphantly at us, his face young and untroubled, and my heart flipped to think of my grandfather making a similar trip at a similar age, except he wasn't on a day trip to a museum and there was no prospect of a proper portion of Yorkshire-born-and-bred fish and chips once the tour was over. When my grandfather reached the coalface his day was just beginning. I looked from my dad to my son, three generations of male Parkinsons, and was humbled by what my grandfather had suffered to make all that we have possible.

When I said that my grandfather wouldn't have had any idea what he would do on his first day it is because mining is not just one job. It is made up of a number of interlocking disciplines that are all required to ensure that the men get to the coalface, the air remains breathable, the coal gets to the top and the whole thing doesn't flood, collapse or plunge into darkness. Even with technological advances, the restrictions of the environment meant machines could only do so much, and throughout its history mining remained massively labour-intensive and dependent upon human endeavour.

At the sharp end of this enterprise were the 'hewers' at the coalface, of which, by the time my grandfather started work, his father Sammy was one. Hewing in those days was not just a matter of brute strength. It required manual dexterity, the skills of a contortionist, not being claustrophobic and no little brain power to ensure that no matter how tight the face was, how narrow the seam, the coal came out in manageable chunks and the whole coalface or rock wall in which it was embedded didn't come down on top of them. They were like muscular geologists.

Once the coal was out, that was just the start of a very long process involving teams of men working at specific tasks. 'Fillers' loaded the coal, with shovels and forks, into

A hewer's workplace for eight hours a day, six days a week.

tubs or onto mechanical conveyors. 'Putters', by a combination of human effort, ponies and mechanised haulage, moved the coal along roadways created by 'stonemen' to the shaft bottom, where the tubs would be placed in cages and wound up to the surface by steam or electrical power.

Alongside all this was the continuous work required to maintain the roadways to ensure ease of access to the coalface and the smooth running of haulage and the need for efficient ventilation, which meant that continuity of production throughout the mine of the hewers, the putters, the stonemen and their various assistants also depended on mechanics, fitters, electricians, general labourers, pony minders and many others. Add to that the administrative level of clerks and the management structure of 'undermanagers' and 'deputies', and you have in size, organisation and cooperation of effort what amounts to a human anthill. A dirty, noisy, dangerous human anthill.

On his first day my grandad would have reported to the clerks, who would sign him on, give him a lamp and set him to work. Most likely he would have ended up being assigned to work in the 'screening sheds', large buildings containing huge metal conveyor belts that carried the coal that had been recently mined, ready for any stones or rocks to be picked out. It was so unbearably noisy and dusty that you could hardly see the coal you were meant to be sorting. No training was given, there were no safety instructions or equipment like googles, ear defenders or masks. Just a bad-tempered, foul-mouthed shed manager to give you 'on job training' by threatening all sorts of appalling violence if you slacked off or made a mistake. It was an initiation into the job of mining that gave the new recruit little doubt as to his status and the working conditions he would have to endure. A young man on his first day must have thought, 'If it's like this up here, what on earth is it like underground?'

The sorting shed was at one and the same time a baptism of fire and a sad elegy for miners. In his fascinating book *Austerity Britain*, about the dreary post-war years my father grew up in, David Kynaston quotes a fifteen-year-old Arthur Scargill on his first day in the screening sheds. It was an experience that helped shape his political sensibility and sense of mission and perhaps explains why, despite being a divisive figure even among miners, Scargill was a strong favourite of my grandfather:

The place was so full of dust you could barely see your hands, and so noisy you had to use sign language. When it came to snap time, your lips were coated in black dust . . . There were two sorts of people in the section:

us, and disabled rejects of society. I saw men with one arm and one leg, men crippled and mentally retarded. I saw people who should never have been working, having to work to live . . . on that first day I promised myself I would try one day to get things changed.

My grandfather's first foray underground would probably have been in the company of a pit pony. Again no training was given, but he would simply have been directed to the stables, where the stable master would tell him to go into a stall and get the pony harnessed and ready for work. For my grandad and his fellow newbies, it would have been a relief to discover that in many cases the ponies were so inured to the work that they simply walked into the harness of their own accord and set off to the pithead, with the bemused young recruit trailing in their wake.

These ponies were not the ones you see gambolling in the New Forest or on Dartmoor, but strong, fearless, short-tempered types who would most likely take your arm off at the elbow if you offered them an apple. These were the poor creatures my dad used to watch from his bedroom window as they celebrated their annual holiday from the mine by running around the field crashing into each other while their eyes adjusted to the bright sunshine.

Pit pony and driver: 'my grandfather's first foray underground'.

The ponies were used to bring the coal to the surface in large tubs, with boys like my grandfather acting as drivers. The ponies' strength, endurance and stature made them essential to the productivity of the mine and it was made clear to the young drivers that the ponies were of far greater importance than them and that it was not advisable to return a pony with any cuts or bruises or to be caught riding them, not that that dissuaded too many of the boys from taking the chance to play the role of an underground Billy the Kid on their way to the coalface.

*   *   *

There were other underground jobs that kids of my grandfather's age would have been assigned. 'Lamping' involved taking safety lamps from the lamp room at the pithead to the colliers working on the face, often walking bent over for a mile or more; 'door trapping' meant sitting alone for eight hours by the single light of a lamp, opening and closing ventilation doors as and when miners needed to come through.

Having earned his stripes in these various roles, along with a few scars, by the age of eighteen or nineteen my grandfather would have begun his life as a hewer or, in the more common parlance of the day, a 'collier', alongside his father. I will not attempt to depict a typical day's work but simply quote George Kemp, a South Yorkshire miner who worked underground between 1934 and 1983, who features in Brian Elliott's *Yorkshire Mining Veterans: In Their Own Words*, a book that has been crucial in keeping my thoughts about my grandfather's life as a miner on the straight and narrow.

Like my grandfather, George Kemp was left with breathing difficulties associated with inhaling coal dust all his working life. In typical miners' fashion, he downplays the experience, but I advise you to read his account with the following facts in mind: all that he describes would have been done in near darkness, amid filth and choking dust, sometimes knee-deep in water and barely clothed because of the searing heat.

I progressed to become a collier when I was nineteen. The . . . seam was about two foot six inches to two foot eight inches in height . . . You worked on your knees. Getting to your work place, you each had ten yards of coal, about fourteen tons to shift. This was a stint. You carried an oil lamp, and later an electric one, also a pick, shovel and hammer. You got rid of the gummings [waste coal] so that it would be higher to work in . . . A nog-end [short wooden wedge] was placed under the coal to keep it up. By ten o'clock [snap time] you felt buggered but three or four slices of bread and fat would revive you. We did not usually leave the face, though we sometimes took five minutes to go . . . to have a stretch. Going to the toilet? Well, you used to have to do it where you were, shovel it into the gob and cover it with coal. You could not do anything else. Some might do it on a shovel and put it on the belt but this was not fair on the lads working on the screens!

The physical and mental toll this kind of work took is revealed in another miner's account, featured in Barry Supple's *History of the British Coal Industry*, Vol 4.

> I soon found that a different kind of strength was needed than the one I had developed. My legs became cramped, my arms ached, and the back of my hands had the skin rubbed off by pressing my knee against them to force the shovel under the coal. The dust compelled me to cough and sneeze, while it collected inside my eyes and made them burn and feel sore. My skin was smarting because of the dust and flying bits of coal. The end of that eight hours was very soon my fondest wish . . . How glad I was to drag my aching body towards that circle of daylight! I had sore knees and was wet from the waist down. The back of my right hand was raw and my back felt the same. My eyes were half closed because of the dust and my head was aching where I had hit it against the top, but I had been eight hours in a strange, new world.

This unpleasant, uncomfortable labour was undertaken by my grandad for eight hours a shift, six days a week, and what is forgotten is that the journey to work was in itself akin to walking up and down a small mountain before you started. Many would walk two or three miles to the pit and then travel another mile underground, crouched over, picking their way around pit props and railway sleepers to get to the coalface. Then and only then would their shift start and they would get paid. The return from work may have been done at a slightly quicker pace, in anticipation of home comforts, but it would have been with tired, aching limbs and, in the absence of pithead baths in many of the mines, often in filthy, soggy clothes.

Miners wait for survivors of an accident underground.
The looks on their faces say it all.

It is not an exaggeration to state that each time my grandfather went to work he was putting his life on the line. Until 1947, when nationalisation of the mining industry standardised working conditions and brought in properly enforced health-and-safety practices, mining was not only a dirty but an incredibly hazardous job.

To the public this was not always obvious, because it was only the pit disasters causing mass loss of life, not the one or two that were killed or horrifically maimed on a regular basis, that got reported and brought the dangerous nature of mining to the public consciousness. But when my grandfather was working, he and his workmates were in grave danger every time they began a new shift, a danger that was brought home to my grandfather when he was part of a rescue squad that helped dig his own father out of a collapsed seam. His father escaped with cuts to his head and when they healed they formed a series of criss-crossing blue scars caused by the coal dust trapped in the wound. My dad found these fascinating as a child, but they were also a stark reminder of how much being a miner was a risk to life and limb.

Giving evidence to a Court of Inquiry on Wages in 1924, the president of the Miners' Federation of Great Britain did not pull any punches:

You know the terrible dangers in our industry, the large numbers of men and boys killed and maimed every year. In 1923, 212,256 men received injuries disabling them for more than seven days, and in addition 1,297 were fatally injured . . . Every working day more than five persons were killed. Every five hours the clock round a life was lost. Every 215,000 tons of coal raised was stained with the crimson of one man's blood. Every working day 850 men and boys were injured . . . Try and visualise this great army of bruised and broken humanity . . . Marshal them in one huge procession, four men in a rank, each 1½ yards apart, and you get a procession of injured men stretching a distance of 45 miles. Every 15 yards of that tragic march you would have an ambulance conveying a man who was seriously injured, and every 61 yards a hearse. This is part of the miners' wages; part of the price he pays in the struggle with natural forces, that the people may have coal.

If you were lucky enough to survive your time as a miner and emerged with all your limbs intact and just a few battle scars to boast about over a pint, it was, however, unlikely you had escaped scot-free from your dance with Old King Coal. There were long-term problems that all miners, to a lesser or greater degree, carried into their retired lives, such as crippling arthritis of the joints and an awful condition caused by operating in dim light called 'miner's nystagmus', or in common parlance 'dancing eyes': rapid involuntary movements of the eyes that affected the ability to focus and could cause serious, irreparable balance issues. Many suffered hearing damage and many acquired silent, debilitating, sometimes fatal lung conditions caused by breathing in fine particles of rock and coal dust.

Recognition that these conditions, in particular lung conditions, were caused by coal mining took about as long as the tobacco industry took to admit that a cigarette didn't help with clearing the airways but actually killed you. Working unprotected in a dusty, dirty environment destroyed my grandfather's lungs and was a major contributory factor to his ill health in later life and premature death. The link between lung disease and the working conditions of miners had first been identified in 1943. Yet it took until 1999 for a £2 billion compensation case to be finally agreed for ex-miners who had suffered disability or premature death because of lung disease acquired in what the Energy Minister John Battle described as 'some of the worst conditions in the world'.

*   *   *

To be fair and to try and give balance – although I always find it slightly difficult to do so given what I have discovered about how, from its earliest days until the modern era, this industry so badly and baldly exploited its workforce, only to drop them like a hot potato when their usefulness disappeared – if you sink a large hole into an environment that is not designed to sustain human life and would really rather you didn't disturb the position it has happily, a few bouts of restlessness aside, settled into over a few millennia, then there are going to be a couple of issues you will be faced with which won't crop up if you're milling cotton in the Derwent Valley. By its nature, deep-shaft mining for any raw material will always be a hazardous and arduous undertaking. This was particularly true in my grandad's era, when the whole enterprise relied predominantly upon human muscle in a harsh and unforgiving environment. Having said that, more should have been done to alleviate the working conditions and danger to life that existed when my grandfather worked at Grimethorpe.

What made the situation far worse for him and his workmates than it should have been was the seemingly total disregard for human life that, for the most part, the mine owners adopted when they discovered that their prime hunting land contained something far more valuable than a few thousand plump breasts of pheasant. Until nationalisation, all mines were owned by the landowners upon whose land the coal was discovered and the mine was sunk. Consequently, the relationship between mine owner and miners never developed much beyond the feudal, with the miners expected to tug their forelock and whistle a happy tune like the seven dwarfs going off to work, and if they dared whistle a different tune that the mine owner didn't like, they would find the pit gates locked and the family larder empty until they slunk back to work like beaten dogs.

None of the industries that were forged in the white heat of the Industrial Revolution was a workers' paradise in the early days, but the mining industry for most of its history in terms of safety and employment regulation lagged behind others, mainly because of its peculiar nature. Coal deposits in England were often in remote, sparsely populated areas. Once the Industrial Revolution began to take hold and the demand for coal grew, villages sprang up around the new mines, but their remote locations meant they were often isolated from the outside world, a situation compounded by the fact that any transport links were, quite deliberately, solely designed to get men to the pit or coal to the markets.

The result was that these communities were cut off. They became inward-looking and focused on one thing: coal. Coal was everything. Work was about coal, village life was organised around coal, your existence was due to coal. It is not a stretch to see that in such circumstances these newly minted population centres were like depositories of 'slave' labour for the shiny new profitable plaything of the lord of the manor, who also benefited from the lack of public interest and therefore proper scrutiny. In many ways that is understandable. How can public interest be piqued if the industry exists in isolated places, with 80 per cent of the work taking place underground?

To the man in the street, a miner was a figure shrouded in mystique and for that reason disconcerting. One of the inspectors for the Sankey Commission remarked that even to his own family a mineworker could appear like 'a disturbing spirit from the underworld'. A miner seen in public after a shift, with his face obscured by dirt and coal dust, could be a forbidding figure.

The only time the light was shone into the darkness was in the event of catastrophic accidents, which certainly drove crucial overdue reforms, but then the inspectors moved on and the light was turned off and the general populace went back to their everyday life blissfully unaware that the problems underneath their feet had not been solved; a mere plaster had been applied to a gaping wound.

Not that the miners welcomed too much scrutiny. They didn't demand sympathy. They didn't see themselves as helpless victims or welcome the intercession of outsiders, even those with their best interests at heart. Quite the opposite. The nature of the work and the isolation of the communities bred within miners a unity of spirit and a non-conformist approach to life, both in terms of religious thought and personal philosophy, that engendered a sense of superiority over those who had never been underground, a wariness of anyone outside their communities and an antipathy towards authority figures, particularly those who tried to tell them how to do things differently. Miners were a proud, insular, feisty bunch with a strong shared identity and a disinclination to take a backward step. They didn't need help in fighting their cause; they were quite capable of doing that by themselves and were never going to be supine in their dealings with the bosses or the national government.

When they formed the Miners' Federation of Great Britain in 1888 they became the most powerful and influential force in the British Labour movement and party for many decades and the battle lines were drawn for a conflict with the powers that be. The early years of the twentieth century saw a series of industrial disputes and bitter lock-outs that confirmed in the minds of the owners, the government officials and the newspapers of the time the miners' reputation as a troublesome, anti-authoritarian force. But these turned out to be just the opening exchanges in the most febrile and seismic period in British coal mining history, which began with the Great War and which my grandfather lived and worked through.

Between 1914 and 1918 the demand for coal went through the roof and in order to guarantee national production without the threat of local disputes derailing the war effort, the mines had been brought into public ownership. Mining also became a reserved occupation, free from the army draft. But there was a choice. There were many 'Pals Battalions' from mines who joined up and their handiwork can be seen in the gaping holes left in the battlefields of France and Belgium caused not by shells but by blown-up mine workings dug under the German trenches by mining conscripts. The mud, mayhem and murder of Flanders Field against the dirt, darkness and danger of Grimethorpe. Some choice. But the ones that stayed were just as heroic as the ones that went singing to their death in the open air.

As the Treaty of Versailles was being signed these subterranean war heroes were determined to drive home the advantages gained because of their crucial role in the war effort. A Triple Alliance of the Miners' Federation of Great Britain, the National Transport Workers' Federation and the National Union of Railwaymen lobbied the government to maintain the better pay and working conditions that the miners had enjoyed during the war under public ownership. Following the 1919 Sankey Commission report, it did seem that this would be the case, but then the government reneged on their promise and returned the mines to their former owners, without any concessions, probably in a deal done over a glass of port in the reading room of White's club in St James's.

The miners called a strike in 1921 which, if the Triple Alliance had held, would have crippled the country, but the government drove a wedge between the three trade unions and the transport workers and the railwaymen broke ranks, while the miners, including my grandfather, were starved back to work in coalfields that were owned and operated on pre-war conditions. And as my grandfather laboured at the coalface and the world economy started to wobble, the wages slipped to such a level that the miners went on strike again and this time the TUC and its members came out in solidarity, in the General Strike of 1926. But as in 1921, they were to be left isolated and were forced back to work as the strike crumbled under government intransigence, weak public support, the use of volunteers and the encouragement of strike-breakers that kept the buses running, the docks unloading, the trains chugging, while the mines remained idle.

Finally, in 1929, the charging bull started breaking things in the Wall Street china shop and the worst economic

Miners returning to work after the failed strike of 1926.

depression that had ever been known gripped the world and turned the coalfields of South Yorkshire into areas of Hogarthian misery. Throughout all this the miners' demands and actions were treated with suspicion, aggression and contempt. The attitude of the ruling class of the time can be summed up in a reaction from Lady Astor, the first female MP, who when told of the miners' threat to strike in 1936 said, 'What do those earthworms want now?' I'm not sure even Marie Antoinette could have been quite so cruelly dismissive.

My grandfather lived and worked through all this, and yet you wouldn't have thought so if you talked to him about his life as a miner. But this era of broken promises, false dawns and extreme hardship shaped the collective psyche of every man who worked underground. No wonder they became politicised, no wonder they became at times militant.

My generation witnessed the social upheavals of the 1970s and 1980s and the miners seared themselves into our consciousnesses during the strikes of the 1980s. As we saw families being torn apart, virtual martial law being enforced on the streets of mining towns and Margaret Thatcher adding insult to injury by calling the miners 'the enemy within', it was simple for a young mind like mine, easily swayed by tied-up-with-string political theories, to see the miners as the vanguard in a necessary class war.

In reality, they became pawns in a high-stakes game between a charismatic trade unionist in Scargill, who saw a chance to realise his Socialist agenda, and a prime minister hell-bent on revenge for the humiliation heaped on the Heath administration by the miners' strike of the early 1970s. What was really happening in front of our eyes was the exploitation, for differing ends, of the bitterness and rage that had been brewed in the hearts and shared consciousness of every miner by an interwar period of high unemployment, declining wages and a constant, dismissive patrician attitude towards them.

Miners have never been 'a disturbing spirit', an 'earthworm', a 'rat' or an enemy of anyone. What they have always been is 'the forgotten people' and when in 2015 the last pit at Hatfield Main Colliery in South Yorkshire was closed, no one mourned the passing of an industry that in its short history had helped forge the modern world but left generations of broken men in its wake. They've buried and beautified the scars on the landscape, but the human cost and the national shame of our treatment of the miners is an open sore.

* * *

By the time the Second World War arrived and mining again became state-controlled and a steady source of employment, my grandfather had begun his first reluctant step up the management ladder. His rank during the war was 'miner corporal below ground' and he was living at 10 Moorland Terrace, Cudworth, with his wife Freda Rose (née King) and their four-year-old son Michael.

A 'miner corporal' worked for the 'deputy', who was the underground supervisor. When the war ended and a country 'fit for heroes' was being constructed, the mines were nationalised and the job of mining became more equitably regulated, in terms of both safety and employment conditions. My grandmother quite liked the idea of her husband securing the better pay, holiday entitlement and other benefits that a deputy could now enjoy and, with the same vigour that she drove my dad to achieve, she cajoled and convinced her husband to take the exams. Despite not really wanting to become a manager, he passed and became a deputy at Grimethorpe pit and my dad and his mum literally and figuratively went off to the movies.

In many ways this was the most difficult time in my grandfather's career. He, as a deputy, was a link between the men and the management and he endured pressure from above and gentle and sometimes not so gentle resistance from below from men with whom he had shared a seam. As ever, he endured it with stoicism and good humour. He spent more than forty years working in a job and living through a time that would have left both physical and mental scars, would have chipped away at the most resilient, would have pushed his endurance to the limit, but it never came close to breaking his spirit nor dulling his *joie de vivre*. He wasn't alone. Miners, when observed in daylight, are, as you will see in the next chapter, a rare breed.

My grandfather's childhood was cut short by the demands of a home life that, as for most families in mining communities of that time, was a case of needs must and making increasingly frayed ends meet. As a consequence, the major influence that shaped him as a person was the mine. His father in a perverse way was Old King Coal, his family the hewers, putters, fillers and all who bravely shared the Stygian gloom with him. Neither my dad nor I would have lasted a day in those shoes.

Like father, like son? At the same age that my grandfather was tying up the laces of his pit boots, my dad was doing up the buttons on his grammar school blazer. Two men separated by different opportunities, different experiences, and yet, as my father recalls in the next chapter, they found each other on the sports field.

CHAPTER 4

LIKE FATHER, LIKE SON

'There is always one moment in childhood when the door opens and lets the future in.'

Graham Greene, *The Power and the Glory*

A cricket team assembled and captained by my
father to take on all comers.

I HAVE HAD THE PRIVILEGE FOR nearly fifty years of living close to one of the most picturesque and idyllic village cricket grounds in the country. It's also one of the oldest – they were playing a form of cricket there a few years before Captain Phillip disembarked his desperate cargo at Botany Bay. If ever Steven Spielberg decides to make a movie about the noble game, he should look no further than the greensward of Maidenhead and Bray. In the late 1960s I was living in Windsor and playing my cricket at a local village called Datchet when, quite by chance, I was invited to play a game at Bray. It was love at first sight and, despite being very happy and settled in our Windsor home, this was enough incentive for me to immediately begin looking for a house nearby.

Maidenhead and Bray Cricket Club has seen not only the twilight of my cricketing career but also the debuts, triumphs and disasters of my three boys, and on the occasions when different generations of Parkinsons were on the cricket field together, I was transported back to the less salubrious cricket grounds of my youth and my experience of playing with my father. One such occasion is remembered in an article I wrote in 1974, on the eve of the announcement of the Ashes touring party to Australia.

Maidenhead and Bray Extras XI – which is a polite way of describing the third team – was at one time in danger of being overrun by Parkinsons. There were two of us in the team – myself and Andrew, then a fourteen-year-old – with two others, Nicholas (ten) and Michael (six), operating the scoreboard. Mrs Parkinson was often the sole spectator, and what is more, John William Parkinson, my old man and chieftain of the tribe, was constantly threatening a comeback as an umpire. If this had happened, he would have been an umpire with a unique outlook on the job.

For instance, he was the only umpire I knew who constantly offered advice to the bowlers. Thus every delivery was followed by a 'Pitch 'em up' or 'Blow him a bouncer' or 'Get thi' bloody hair cut'. Also, he was one of the few umpires of my experience who appealed along with the bowler. Many's the time he leapt in the air and joined with the bowler in an ear-shattering appeal for lbw, leaving the departing batsman with serious doubts about the supposed impartiality of the adjudicator.

Once he appealed for a catch behind the wicket and discovered to his chagrin, after his cry had echoed round the field, that his had been the only voice raised in anguish. As the fielders and a startled batsman regarded him with awe, he straightened his tie, cleared his throat and said, 'Not out, you silly old bugger.'

Maidenhead and Bray Extras XI, however, was spared the experience of having my old man as umpire. He delayed his comeback until the party to tour Australia at the time was announced. He lived in hope that they would send for him as baggage man or the like, or that they would consult him in matters of team selection.

He had had his team selected for some time. It was:

D. B. Close (Somerset) captain
R. Illingworth (Leicestershire) vice-captain
G. Boycott (Yorkshire) deputy vice-captain
B. Wood (Lancashire)
J. Balderstone (Leicestershire)
J. H. Wardle (Cambridgeshire)
J. Laker (BBC TV Centre)
F. S. Trueman (Batley Variety Club)

Plus the rest of the current Yorkshire side. He felt certain that this team would conquer the world.

However, all that is by the by and nothing whatsoever to do with the Maidenhead and Bray third team, except for the fact that, by playing in the same team as my son, I was reliving the time a million summers ago when I played in the same team as my old man.

In those days he was coming to the end of a career as a fast bowler of real pace and hostility, during which time he had achieved a reputation which made him as welcome on the playing fields of South Yorkshire as a family of moles. He captained the second team and collected around him a gang of raggy-arsed miners' sons which he turned into a cricket team – and a good one at that.

Under his critical gaze we learned the basics of the loveliest of games, like play back, play forward and never hook or cut until the chrysanthemums have flowered. He taught us the game's intricacies and mysteries, like lifting the seam on the ball with a thumbnail, maintaining its shine with Brylcreem, and the tactical virtue of the bouncer followed by the yorker. 'One to make his eyes water, the other to knock his pegs over,' he'd say.

He was a stickler for doing things properly, for people looking the part. He would not allow anyone in his team who was what he considered to be 'improperly dressed', which in his eyes would be someone wearing black socks or brown plimsolls. At this time there were a good number of youths in our team who didn't own the proper equipment – their parents either didn't care or couldn't afford it – but no one ever took the field in Father's team unless he looked like a proper cricketer. He insisted on all of us going to the wicket correctly padded and protected. In those days it was commonplace to see a cricketer wearing one pad and no batting gloves, and a protector was something only wicketkeepers and pansies wore. Father would have none of it, and would even admonish youngsters on opposing teams who came to the wicket less than adequately protected.

If the youngster wearing one pad refused his advice to return to the pavilion and put the other pad on, he would take the ball and aim it at the unprotected leg. He was still accurate enough to hit it and quick enough to make his victim wish he had taken his advice.

Eventually we grew up under his wing and became a team of young men. Then we broke up and went our different ways, some into the first team, some to different clubs and higher leagues. I went to Barnsley and the old man retired to come and watch me play, standing behind the bowler's arm, wincing at my foolishness in cutting when the chrysanthemums were a long way from flowering.

I used to laugh with him and at him a lot, marking him down as a character and thinking he represented a generation and a lifestyle that was totally different from mine. He was, I reckoned, a man I'd never be.

Then when I started to play with my son I had the feeling that I was seeing a familiar landscape, the sense that I had been there before. When Andrew threw the new ball to the bowler on the bounce I said, 'Up, up, keep the bloody thing up,' and my father's voice came echoing down the years.

When he made a brilliant stop I grinned like an idiot and when he let the ball through his legs I felt like hitting him with the stump. In one game he had to go out and block for a couple of overs to save the game, and I told him how to play the off-spinner with bat and pad together, bat angled down and straight down the line.

I took up my position by the sightscreen, ready to play every ball with him, and damn me if he didn't walk down the track to the first ball and drive it through mid-on. It was not what I had told him to do, and I semaphored my displeasure. As I did so I saw the stumper looking at me in an odd way and having a word with my son. Does this sound familiar?

I knew what the wicketkeeper was saying to my son because although times have changed and everyone in our team wears proper pads and protectors and no one plays in brown plimsolls, the fundamentals remain the same.

The fact is me and my old man are peas from the same pod, like father like son, and what I learned at his knee about the most beautiful of games is part of a heritage that I found myself passing on to my sons. I stood by that sightscreen and didn't care what the stumper was thinking. In that precious moment I was a man contented and fulfilled.

Because of the far-sighted social and educational reforms of the ambitious and dynamic post-war Labour government, my generation were the first working-class men and women who were able to peek over the wall at the secret garden that the class system had kept locked away from us for so long. The lucky ones of our generation would go on to have lives and experiences that were so different to our parents' as to make us have as much in common with them as the human race would have with a charabanc of Martians arriving here on a day trip. Despite this, we still carried with us the imprint of their personality, the values they treasured, the prejudices they harboured, shaped in very different times to the one we were living through, and also, if we were lucky, the benign influence of a man like my father.

The articles I have written about my father are not whimsical imaginings but my most cherished remembrances of a man who was neither brutal nor embittered – though, as we learned in the last chapter, he had every right to be – and never once made me feel frightened, rejected or lost. I struck it lucky. And yet I can't quite get out of my mind the phrase that described a miner in his home as being seen as 'a disturbing spirit from the underworld'. There is no sense in which my father was 'disturbing', but there is no doubt there was an unbridgeable gap between us, a hole in our understanding of each other that can only be put down to what he did for a living.

Miners, like many who work in dangerous, demanding jobs that stretch every nerve and sinew, often choose, as a way of preventing the whole thing from overwhelming them, to be reticent to the point of inarticulateness about what they do on a daily basis. If they do talk about their work, it's in a bluff, no-nonsense way, couched in a language and a form of expression that is very much their own. By their nature miners, therefore, are a separate tribe who receive no nation-wide rounds of applause, alas, no national memorials to remember the dead and injured, no headlines in newspapers extolling their virtues – often quite the opposite – and therefore no sense that what they do is in any way appreciated.

So to me a large part of my father's life was, until we unpicked it for this book, a mystery. And he was happy that it should remain one. He chose to leave his job at the pit gate. He refused to bring back an ounce of what he did for eight hours a day and disrupt the domestic idyll my mother and I represented for him, and in no way did he want his son to look up to his father because of tales of derring-do in the underworld.

There were far more important reasons to look up to him than his bravery and dexterity with a pick and shovel. My father found solace in doing anything that made him forget his work with as much gusto as he could. Many of his work-mates, sadly, were unable to cope with the demands the mine placed upon body and spirit and took to drink as a way out. Some would turn inward and visit their misery upon those closest to them. But my father decided that the best cure for all ailments was a good dose of fresh air and an even bigger injection of sporting contest, in particular cricket, and he couldn't quite believe he had a son who shared his passion.

The cricket pitch is where we grew to know and love each other, where I absorbed the part of him that became part of me. In truth, given the demands of his job, the only place we had time to meet as father and son was on the cricket pitch, and it was the perfect place to make his acquaintance. I have always said that you can learn a lot about a person's character from the way they play sport, and in my father's case it became quite clear that he was a one-off. What's also clear is that some of what he passed on to me he had learnt from his father. Here's an article I wrote about the time he played with his father Sammy in a local knock-out that was featured in *Parkinson's Lore*.

To have played cricket and never taken part in a knock-out competition is like joining the Army and never hearing a shot fired in anger. Knock-out cricket is designed to bring the worst out of players and spectators alike. It gives off that most delicious of cricket perfumes: the heady whiff of crushed grass and skulduggery.

My old man adored knock-out cricket. Being the sort of player who could turn a gentle game of beach cricket into something resembling the landing at Iwo Jima, he relished the tense and often violent atmosphere of knock-out cricket. Much of the excitement at these games comes from the spectators whose normal ration of pride in the local team is supplemented by the fact that they have ten bob on the game with the local bookie.

My old man told a lovely story of the time he played his first knock-out game. His father was a big betting man and was well pleased when the opposition was bowled out for 42.

It seemed a walkover for my old man's team, so much so that when he went to look at the batting order the skipper had only put down four names and said to my dad, 'Off tha' goes. We shan't need thee.'

Fortunately he stuck around long enough to see his team collapse to the extent that when he went out to bat at No 11 his side were 20 for nine wickets and needed 23 to win. As he went down the pavilion steps he was the object of much excellent advice from the betting fraternity, none more pithy than that offered by his father, who said, 'If tha' gets out before we've beaten them, I'll thump thi' ear'ole.'

Basing his innings on this sound advice, my old man managed to keep his end up while the batsman at the other end scored the runs to win the game.

The rejoicing was great and my old man was later downing a hero's pint in a nearby hostelry when he was approached by a local who said:

'Spending thi' collection money, then?'

'What collection?' said my old man.

'That what thi' father organised after tha'd won t'game for us. Collected about five quid on thi' behalf.'

Father swallowed his pint and dashed to the ground, where he met his old man lurching gently away from the bar.

'Where's my collection, then?' he said.

'Supped it,' said his old man, burping loudly.

When I came along, my father had decided that his ambitions for me were bigger than the chance to sup any collection money I won and that meant creating a cricketer good enough to wear the White Rose of Yorkshire. Apart from that achievement meaning he would become father to a local legend, I'm also sure part of him believed this to be the only way he could think of that would ensure I didn't walk to the pit with him one day.

Below we have selected a few of my articles which reveal the many ways my father taught me the intricacies and techniques of the game he loved and how we became, at least on the cricket field, like father, like son.

When I was born my paternal grandmother tried very hard to have me called Melbourne because MCC had just won a Test match there. Fortunately my mother, a southerner of great common sense, would have none of it. Not so my father who, being a Yorkshireman and therefore cricket mad, was torn between Herbert (Sutcliffe), Percy (Holmes) or Hedley (Verity). Mother settled for Michael and would not budge. That was the only concession my old man made during the next twenty years which he devoted to producing a son who would one day play for Yorkshire.

When I was five years old, he bought me a cricket bat. The blade was creamy, the handle red, and it was the best bat I ever possessed.

I picked it up for the first time and stood in the approved position, left shoulder pointed down the wicket, left toe cocked in honour of George Roberts, the local big hitter, who at the time I considered the best batsman in the world. My old man patiently took the bat from me, turned me so my right shoulder pointed down the wicket and nodded in satisfaction. Thus, a left-handed bat was created against nature's whims.

I didn't question the move at the time, but later the old man explained everything. 'No bowler likes left-handers, lad. Remember that and think on that you've got a head start.' As a bowler himself he reckoned he knew what he was talking about. He hated bowling at 'caggy handers'.

When he finished bowling and became captain of our second team he worked on the simple philosophy that the more left-handed batsmen he could discover or invent, the better our chances of victory. He proved his point by winning the championship with a team which included nine left-handed bats, four natural, five manufactured. He took great delight in the freakish nature of his team and loved observing the mounting incredulity of his opponents as left-handed bat followed left-handed bat to the wicket. After the first half dozen, the opposing captain would often turn to the old man, lurking on the boundary edge, and say, 'Ayup, skipper. 'Ow many more bloody caggy 'anders siree?'

At eleven I was playing in the team he captained, a child among men, a pimple among muscles. But I received no quarter because the old man would not have it.

On my way to another post-mortem with my father.

Considering the atrocious wickets we played on and the psychotic bowlers we faced, that I survived that period intact was due to my own fleet-footedness and not, as my father used to insist, to the rumour that God protected prospective Yorkshire cricketers. He based this on the fact that He was born just outside Barnsley.

After every game came the post-mortem, the old man dissecting every innings I played, advising, criticising, stuffing my young head with the game's folklore. There was nothing selfish in this. He would have done the same for any kid my age because he couldn't stand the game being played badly. Only once did he use my tender years to his advantage. We were playing at a ground near Barnsley on a wicket which gave every impression of having been prepared by a mechanical trench digger. We got our opponents out for about 40 and were in trouble at 24 for seven when the old man joined me at the wicket. He came to me and said, 'Just keep your head down and leave the rest to me.'

He walked to the non-striker's end and immediately engaged in conversation with their fast bowler, who had taken five wickets and put two of our players into the casualty ward. As the fast bowler walked back to his mark the old man walked with him.

'Long run for an off-spinner,' he said as they walked side by side.

'Wheer's tha' think tha's going?' said the fast bowler, stopping on his walk back.

'Wi' thee,' said the old man.

'Aye oop, umpire,' said the bowler. 'Can't tha' stop him?'

The umpire shook his head.

'Nowt in t'rules says he can't walk alongside thee, lad,' said the umpire.

At the end of his walk back the bowler turned and began his run to the wicket and the old man kept pace with him stride for stride. Halfway to the wicket the bowler stopped.

'Aye oop, umpire, can't tha' see what he's doing?' said the bowler to the umpire at square leg.

'Aye, he's running alongside thee, lad, but there's nowt to say he can't,' said the umpire.

The bowler, shadowed everywhere by my old man, completely lost his head and bowled three balls which nearly killed third slip. After the third he turned to my old man and addressed him in what I understood to be called 'pit language'. The old man listened for a while and then turned to the umpire and said, 'Did tha' hear that, Charlie?'

'I did that, John William,' said Charlie.

'Does tha' reckon it's fit language for a schoolboy to hear?'

'No,' said Charlie firmly.

'Then we're off and claiming maximum points,' said the old man, before marching from the field.

As we walked off I pointed out that I had heard that kind of language – and worse – before, so why had he taken umbrage?

'Tactics,' he said.

He proved his case by defending his action to the League Committee and being awarded maximum points for a game we hadn't a hope of winning.

In those days there were no friendly fixtures in Yorkshire. The Leagues were the spawning grounds of Yorkshire cricket. They were trawled with a fine mesh and the county missed very little.

I learned a lot from my father, particularly about the art of psychological warfare. He was an expert at illusion, creating uncertainty among his opponents. I remember one day when he introduced a new fast bowler the opposition had never seen before. After the first over their opening bat said to my father, 'By gum, John William, but your new lad's a bit quick.' And my father said, 'He is that. But tha' should have seen him before he got gassed.'

It was tough cricket, as far removed from the romantic image as could be imagined. Where there should have been blue hills in the distance we had muckstacks, instead of deckchairs there were hard wooden benches. The men who sat on them had not come to enjoy themselves. Their job in life was to make the players miserable, to give them some stick.

Youngsters, no matter how young, were given no quarter. It was assumed if you were picked to play in the League you could look after yourself. If you couldn't, then tough. I remember my father being worked over by a young fast bowler who, after hitting him several times, finally offered a smirky, fairly sarcastic 'Sorry'. Whereupon my old man said, 'Nay, don't apologise, lad, it's my turn next.' And he was as good as his word.

Soon after, I left his team to play for Barnsley in the Yorkshire League. This was what decided him to give up the game in order that he might stand behind the bowler's arm coaching his protégé with an extraordinary repertoire of dramatic gestures.

When I batted he would stand by the sightscreen semaphoring his displeasure with a series of anguished body contortions. Marcel Marceau had nothing on my old man. His most dramatic mimes occurred whenever I attempted a late cut. I had a great liking for the shot which my father regarded as being both frivolous and profane. His initial display of displeasure at the shot was a sorrowful shake of the head. This could be augmented by placing his hand on his brow like a man with a severe headache. If I persisted with the shot he would hit his brow with the heel of his hand and stagger around in dramatic fashion like a man who has just been told that his wife has run off with the lodger.

His most spectacular demonstrations always occurred whenever I tried a late cut and missed. He believed firmly with Maurice Leyland that you never late-cut before June and even then only if the moon had turned to green cheese. I once played this shot in a game at Barnsley and, having missed, looked towards the sightscreen, where the old man was going through his customary paroxysm of displeasure. As I watched, the stumper approached me.

'Are tha' watching what I'm watching?' he asked. I nodded.

'I reckon he's having a bloody fit,' said the stumper. 'Does tha' know him?'

'Never met him before in my life,' I said.

Whenever I got near a fifty he couldn't bear to watch and always spent ten minutes in the gents' toilet until the crowd noise informed him that I was either on 50 or out. I went to one fifty by hitting the ball into that very same toilet, where it was fielded by my old man, who came out holding the ball gingerly but looking like a man who had found a gold nugget.

I never told him I didn't want to play cricket for a living. I didn't dare. The truth dawned when I realised a life's ambition and joined the *Guardian* (*Manchester Guardian* as it then was). Delightedly I crossed the Pennines to tell my parents. Mother was really pleased. Father said, 'It's not like playing cricket for Yorkshire.'

He was only half joking because I knew he was proud of me, knew that on the day I left that house to leave the village and not to go to the pit, he was a man content. One of the delights of the latter part of my career was when he was able to come to the *Parkinson* shows and meet the screen idols, mainly female, that had kept him company in the dark of Grimethorpe pit. He was a man of his generation who'd lived a hard life, expected no thanks and had not much truck with inward speculation. As a result he was full of inarticulate pride in me.

As the possibility of me becoming Yorkshire County Cricket Club's latest great hope receded in the time it took

Trueman, Close, Illingworth et al. to dismantle my stumps at the Yorkshire nets, he replaced his semaphoring behind the wicket whilst I was batting with striking up conversations with strangers – even sometimes, to the natural alarm of the person in the neighbouring urinal, in public lavatories – and as skilfully as any live broadcaster turning the conversation to a point where he could casually mention the fact that he was my father.

It was embarrassing for me at the time, but I now look back on it with a smile. He wasn't a boastful man – he was modest to the point of reticence about himself – but he was just bursting with pride. He couldn't tell me, so he told someone else. But he should also have told them that he had played a crucial role in preparing me for one of the highlights of my later career as a talk-show host, the time I met that most singular of men, Muhammad Ali.

Still to this day I'm not quite sure why my father decided I should be a prizefighter. I have pondered the reasons for his ambition to make me a champion pugilist without discovering an answer. He was a peaceful man in that he walked away from any confrontation which might end up in fisticuffs, and yet when I was thirteen or fourteen he bought me a pair of boxing gloves for my birthday, saying he thought it about time I learned how to look after myself.

At that point in my life I had experienced one fight, which took place behind an air-raid shelter with Sonny Shaw, a wiry youth and an evacuee who insulted a girl I was hoping to marry when legally allowed. Our encounter was a bare-fist job and lasted about two minutes until my opponent, who had back-pedalled from the start, without a single punch being exchanged, fell backwards into a pile of bricks and cut his head. Honour was satisfied but without lasting consequence, because my girlfriend married a plumber, leaving me free to marry Ingrid Bergman and whisk her from Hollywood to a two-up two-down I had selected as our marital home situated opposite the main entrance to Barnsley Football Club. When I met Ms Bergman I told her this story and she gave me the kind of worried smile you assemble before enquiring which nursing home you have escaped from.

A time passed without me wearing boxing gloves until the moment arrived when my father decided I should be taught the manly art of self-defence, the sweet science. There was a guy living nearby who had a son of my age whom he had taught to box. The two dads had words and decided it would be a good idea for me to have a similar education. The venue was our lawn, the one with the red wigwam on it, which was a changing room for the two fighters. It was agreed both boxers would take it easy while my opponent's dad gave me the once-over just to see exactly what he had to teach me.

His son Billy was a nice lad, a friend of mine and a tough and respected street fighter. So the bell went and I approached my opponent who, without any preliminary flirting, feinted a left cross and then hit me full on the nose with a meaty right piledriver. Blood flowed. I fell in dramatic fashion and my mother, who had been a disapproving spectator through the kitchen window, started cleaning the flood of blood and mucus emanating from where my nose had been. My father suggested Mr Taylor and son should go home, which they did, leaving the Parkinson family in bloodied disarray.

The consequence of the fight – if you could call it that – was that Mum barred Dad and me from the house and suggested we sleep in the wigwam until we learned some common sense.

It was some time before my dad proposed we satisfy our curiosity about boxing. It was during a visit to a fair in Oxford at which two booth fighters called Randolph and Jackie Turpin offered to take on all comers. There was a way to go before Randolph Turpin would beat Sugar Ray Robinson and became a world champion. When I first saw him as a booth fighter he felled his opponent – a much bigger man – with a blow to the forehead so hard that when the victim moved through the crowd to collect a meagre few quid, he bore a lump on his forehead the size of a large egg.

Some time later, when I was a journalist with *The Guardian*, I tried to interview Randolph Turpin, who at the time was a forgotten casualty of the noble art. He didn't cooperate. He didn't lift his eyes from the comic he was reading. Shortly afterwards he put a gun in his mouth and pulled the trigger.

Much later than that I did a series of interviews with Muhammad Ali, before the consequences of his chosen profession overwhelmed him. Looking back and thinking of the four interviews I did with Ali, the connection is obvious, and it all started with a fight outside a red wigwam in Cudworth organised by my father.

It wasn't just me my father cared for and tried to nurture, occasional bloody noses aside. He was not jealous in his love and affection. As soon as they were born, he turned his attention wholeheartedly onto his grandchildren, and in any team in which I played with him, he was a man who loved a trier. Indeed, he would go out of his way to make them better players, in the hope that they would then take the game as seriously as he did and love it with the same passion, in order to derive the same amount of pleasure as he did when he pulled on his whites for the start of a new cricket season. He was – in the days before teams of specialists and computer analysis arrived – the perfect coach and the ideal captain, not to mention the teaching fraternity's loss. Nurturing yet stern, he innately understood that life lessons can be learned just as well on a sports pitch as anywhere else, and whoever played with him and met him never forgot the experience.

J.P.W. Mallalieu, the MP for Huddersfield from 1945 until the late 1970s, once said, 'Miners rub shoulders with death. They know how to face death . . . and they will not let death spoil life.' That is exactly what my father did every minute he wasn't down the pit. Whether on the sports field, at home, on his allotment or in the company of friends, he grabbed life by the throat. He was constantly full of an irrepressible good humour and optimism. He saw no obstacles in his way, only solutions, and if a problem needed fixing, he saw no reason why he shouldn't be the man to do it. Like the time he once decided to build a garage:

My father was a man who treasured his possessions.

In his sporting days his cricket boots were blancoed to

perfection, his whites were whiter than, and his bat, which must have been used by W.G. Grace, was cleaned and oiled like a new-born child. Similarly, his football boots were dubbined until they were as supple as kid and then polished until they gleamed like shiny black dancing-pumps.

When he bought a car, an ancient and world-weary Triumph, he didn't leave it in the street to spend its final years in the gutter, he built a garage for it. Considering the state of the vehicle, this was something like building a solarium for a corpse. Being blessed with considerable ingenuity but no money, father decided to construct his own garage. The fact that he had built nothing more complicated than a rabbit hutch in no way deterred him.

After assembling a pile of railway sleepers, pit props and orange boxes, he nailed the lot together with six-inch nails and painted the doors green. It would never have won an award for elegance and looked so ramshackle that it afforded much hilarity among the neighbours, but it was, in fact, an overcoat for my father's proudest posses-sion, and that was all he cared about.

What he didn't realise was that I had different uses for his garage and it was to play an important part in my sporting education. In those days when street lamps were our wickets and two coats our goal-posts, the garage became Lord's and Wembley all rolled into one. We chalked three stumps on the doors that were also our goals, and on alternate days, until the soccer season faded and cricket took over, the garage became the focal point of all our fantasies.

It was here that Barnsley won the cup final three years running from 1947 to 1950 and on each occasion I scored the winning goal in extra time. It was here that Len Hutton's record Test score of 364 was surpassed by another young Yorkshireman called Tiger Parkinson who smote Lindwall, Miller et al. all over the county before retiring with a broken bat for an undefeated 527.

The same player was well on the way to surpassing even that mammoth score when there occurred one of those traumatic incidents that so affect the life of the budding sportsman. Swinging hard to leg to hook yet another six, I pivoted around, bat flailing, and hit the corner of the garage, whereupon the whole structure sighed, creaked and fell apart like a pack of cards. My father's anger was increased by the knowledge that his garage had been demolished by the kind of stroke he disapproved of and I had the definite impression that had it been collapsed in the execution of a proper defensive stroke nothing would have been said about it.

We built our next garage out of bricks, knocking down a couple of old air-raid shelters to get the materials, and my penance for a rash stroke was to sit at home when I ought to have been practising my shots, chopping away mortar from bricks that had been built to withstand bombs. The new garage, again constructed by my father without recourse to any professional advice, was so lop-sided that it made the Leaning Tower of Pisa look like Centre Point.

Local brickies would make detours to marvel at the unique skill of someone who could build sloping garages. I was present when one of them, goggling in awe, was approached by my old man. 'What's tha' reckon?' asked Father. The brickie thought for a bit and then said, 'Ah reckon tha' ought to stick to fast bowling.' No matter what the building profession thought about our garage, my old man was determined that it should not be used for purposes other than those for which it was constructed. This meant an end to our practice facilities.

To soften our disappointment the old man persuaded the committee at the cricket club to build a concrete practice strip. The committee agreed on condition that father took no part in its construction and decided that while they were at it they would build a toilet next to the pavilion, several lady members having objected to the sight of grown men standing up against the hedge surrounding the ground trying to look nonchalant and pretending they were bird-nesting.

In our tiny world such a plan constituted an event, and therefore it was decided the new pitch and the toilet should be opened by the chairman of the council. A major problem was finding a net to enclose the practice pitch, and this we achieved by persuading the soccer club to part with one of their goal nets. The fact that a net designed for stopping footballs is not likely to be ideal when used for cricket never occurred to us – until it was too late.

The day before the grand opening, with a full-scale rehearsal for the civic ceremony of our toilet going on nearby, we decided to try out the pitch. I had the honour of taking first strike and, wanting to give it a proper baptism, decided that whatever was bowled at me I was going to give it a go. Unfortunately the first ball was a long hop outside the leg stump and foolishly I played the shot that had already demolished a garage.

I was fully aware of what I was doing, reasoning that the net would stop the ball. It didn't. The fact is a cricket ball will pass through a football net like a draught through an open window. The ball whistled through the net as if it wasn't there, broke the window of the new toilet with a noise like a gunshot and shattered the shiny new flush toilet tank into a thousand pieces.

The civic opening was postponed, and until we'd found the money for a new lav we spent several weeks in the hedges pretending we were bird-nesting. The old man had a theory, that had they let him build the toilet it would have leaned so much that the ball would have missed. That's as may be. All I know is that it was ages before I attempted the hook shot again.

Many years later, playing with another club, I was batting against a bowler who was trundling up what could most generously be described as rubbish. He bowled me a long hop outside the leg stump and I couldn't resist it. I gave it an almighty whack, only to be caught one-handed and brilliantly by a youth standing on the boundary. Had he not been there it would have been a six. Later in the bar the bowler said to me, 'I found thi' weakness.' That was pretty funny. What he didn't know was that with my kind of luck, if the fielder

115

hadn't caught the ball I would most likely have knocked the pavilion down.

My father's irrepressible spirit and desire to shake off the cobwebs of his working life meant that any chance of celebration was enjoyed at full throttle. High days and holidays were an opportunity for my father not only to unveil in all its glory his mischievous and wicked sense of humour, but also to revel in his desire that everyone else should have as good a time as him.

What we used to do for Christmas was share a pig with three or four other families. Throughout the year we would take it in turns to clean and feed it and then, just when we were getting fond of it, my old man and his mates would send for the local gamekeeper, who would slaughter anything for a couple of bob and a pint or two. I can remember standing outside the pig sty – a very small child – tears running down my face at the noise of the carnage inside.

One year someone pinched our pig. They waited until it was fattened and ready for the kill and then spirited it away at dead of night. We never found out who it was but ever after we mounted guard on our pig sty from

November onwards, protecting it from evil, saving it for the slaughterman.

Our Christmases really began when the pig was jointed, jellied, pied, sausaged, rissoled, trottered and shared out among the owners. Looking back, Christmas to my child's mind was a rich stew of smells and sensations. The table groaned, for the one and only day of the year, under the unexpected weight of food, men I only saw in their working clothes and pit muck turned up in tight blue suits and Co-op shoes and aunties with new hairdos seemed suddenly aware of what they'd kept under their pinafores all year long, and the air was heavy with Soir de Paris and the promise of sex.

Our Christmases were divided into three main compartments. Eating and drinking, sporting, and partying. We always used to have the parties at our house, not because it was any bigger than the others in the street but because my old man was the unchallenged party-giver of the entire South Yorkshire coalfield. Virtually teetotal the year round, he broke the rule at Christmas, when a pint of bitter mixed with his extraordinary output of adrenalin made him an uproarious and indefatigable host.

In my father's book there were only two categories of

people, those who could take a joke and those who couldn't. He loved the former and ignored the latter, although to be fair to the latter, you had to be pretty patient and even-tempered to appreciate some of my father's jokes. For instance, his favourite party piece was a game called 'Press it on' which, adapted by Father, was subtitled 'blacking up'.

This involved the unwitting cooperation of one of the guests who was hand-picked each year by Father and asked to come to the party only that Father might play his joke on him. At a suitable time during the evening, when everyone was well bevvied and burping gently, Father would seat his sucker guest on a chair and stand behind him with his back to the coal fire. The other guests would be instructed to form a seated circle along-side the chosen guest.

My old man then explained to the poor sod sitting innocently in front of him that the game was a simple one in which my father would touch the guest's face with his finger and the guest then had to duplicate the touch on his neighbour's face, who would pass it on until it came full circle. The trick was, my father explained, to duplicate the touch absolutely and not to laugh. If, in the opinion of the honoured guest, the fellow players did not duplicate the face touching properly and/or he laughed during the proceedings they would be due a forfeit.

What the victim never realised, of course, was that before Father touched his face he first of all daubed his fingers with soot from the fireback. Years of practice had confirmed that he could completely black a person's face without the victim knowing a thing providing none of the other guests let on. The moment when the victim was given a mirror and came face to face with the appalling mess my father had created was a real test of his good humour and my father's skill at convincing him that he was now a member of an elite club. I saw him perform his trick on about a score of victims and the only time it went wrong was with the local sanitary inspector, who stormed off home and then sent Dad a bill for ruining his white shirt. Father stated he never did like the fellow and said that in any case he was the one that pinched the pig.

To me as a child Christmas was simply a matter of how many points Barnsley took from their three games. It also meant a new pair of football boots or a shirt from a football-daft father. 'Who are you this year?' he'd ask, as I got all togged up at 5 a.m. on Christmas morning. 'George Robledo,' I'd say, and race out of doors to play a game with my imagination under the flickering gas lamps with the windows in the other houses still dark and sleeping.

Christmas games were special. Everything was different. Behind the goal there were more cigars than Woodbines, the bottles of Scotch flickered twixt hip and lips with the lightning speed of a hummingbird's wings and the crowd rustled in its new clothes. The players were affected too; they even looked different. As a boy I imagined the change in countenance was due to the fact that they, like the rest of us, were sprinkled with Christmas stardust.

Later, as the layers of naivety slipped from me, I came to know that they were simply hungover. I first came face to face with the truth during a Christmas game some years ago when a full-back on Barnsley's side played in the most erratic manner. He appeared to be unsteady on his feet and quite unable to decide which side he was on or what he was supposed to be doing. The truth dawned as he ran to take a free kick, missed the ball completely and fell flat on his back. He lay there for a while, feet and arms feebly twitching, until suddenly he was still and at peace.

The crowd regarded all this curiously and silently for

a moment, and then someone yelled, 'Look at 'im, lying there like a roll of bloody lino.' The crowd roared and the trainer grinned sheepishly as he went to work with the smelling salts. Accounting for this unique slice of behaviour, an official communique, issued some time later, said that the full-back had suffered an 'emotional disturbance' before the game and this had affected his play. The old man told me, on the quiet, that the emotional disturbance was caused by the change in the licensing hours at Christmas.

By the time I was old enough to tie the laces on my first pair of football boots, my father had given up playing football and instead filled my head with stories of real and mythical footballing heroes until I was old enough to visit the hallowed turf of Oakwell, home of Barnsley Football Club, and worship at the self-made altar of my own set of heroes. A love of sport and adoration of talent passed down through the generations, except I made a little more money from celebrating my footballing heroes than my father ever did.

I was five years old when I was taken to my first game of football. My father reminds me occasionally that at half-time when he asked me how I liked it I said, 'It's all

A family holiday at Butlin's with neighbours.

right but I think we'll go now.' To which he replied, 'I don't think we will,' thereby making a decision which condemned me to a lifetime of addiction to the game. Out of that first tentative encounter grew a love affair which has lasted until the present without showing the slightest sign of weakening. The name of the lady is Barnsley and through the years – the few good ones, the many lean ones – I have loved her like my favourite blowsy barmaid.

Even now it's easy to switch my mind back to the days when we caught the bus and made the five-mile journey into Barnsley to see the Reds play. The bus was always crowded with men in hairy overcoats and flat caps, smelling of Woodbines and last night's beer. At the station we would join the chattering throng as it surged up the hill and down the dip into the ground. Oakwell, the home of Barnsley Football Club, could not by any stretch of the imagination be called a pleasant spot, but no sight has thrilled me more, before or since, than the sudden view of the ground as we breasted the hill from the bus station and our eyes met the place where our heroes lived. Even now their names are easily remembered, like some familiar prayer: Binns, Harston, Shotton; Logan, Birkenshaw, Asquith; Smith, Cooling, Robledo, Barlow and McGarry. Inside the ground we would head for our favourite spot, to the east of the players' entrance on the terrace. It had been my father's spot ever since he got a rise at the pit which enabled him to move from the back of the goals.

There we would be joined, week in week out, by our little but noisy family of regulars. There was the Maniac, charmingly called because of his towering outbursts of rage which occurred every time the opposition committed a foul. And Wobblygob, a spotty youth who earned his name through a pair of fulsome lips. This unfortunate act of nature was remarked upon most cruelly one

Saturday by a Rotherham fan, who, tiring of the abuse being heaped on his team, turned round and said, 'Tha' could ride a bike round thi' gob.'

Together we shared the infinite pleasures and black despair which any football fan goes through following the fortunes of his team. It was in that same spot, with the view of the muck stacks on the other side, that I stood for years and saw many things both beautiful and ugly, sad and comic, and every Saturday grew more in love with the game. It was here that I first saw Frank Swift, massive and graceful, demonstrate the art of goalkeeping. I remember vividly Swift catching the ball with one hand and holding it above the head of a tiny Barnsley forward who kept jumping for it like a dog for a bone. It was here I saw a stripling youth called Blanchflower spin the first delicate lines of his genius and looking as incongruous as a thoroughbred in a donkey derby. Here too I saw Matthews and Doherty and Carter and Lawton and Mortensen and Shackleton. But great as they were, and glamorous too, I never loved them as much as the nondescripts who made up the Barnsley team throughout the years.

*　　*　　*

Alongside other ghosts of that time past was my father's true sporting hero, Wilson of *The Wizard*, a Yorkshire-born comic-strip hero who had found the secret to an extended life by living in a cave high on the Yorkshire Moors, eating nothing but roots and berries and learning how to slow down his heartbeat. The result was by the time he was reported as missing in action over the English Channel during World War II, as a decorated Spitfire pilot with twenty-five confirmed kills, he was rumoured to be over 200 years old and had already climbed Everest, captained an Ashes-winning cricket team, won the Tour de France on a postman's bike and crossed the Andes barefoot. My father, being a romantic at heart and a lover and teller of improbable stories, saw no reason why he couldn't emulate this fellow Yorkshireman.

There is a huge, deep-rooted tradition of gambling in these parts. Not just the straightforward things like the ponies, pools or the dogs. They will back anything.

Once the old man challenged a local councillor, ten years his junior, to a 100-yard sprint race just because the councillor remarked that the old man appeared short of breath when he came into the tap-room one night. My father bet him ten quid that he couldn't beat him given yards for years. The race was arranged for the following Sunday at a field overlooking the pit where the pre-fabs are now.

When Sunday came just about the whole village turned out. Everyone had some money on the race and the councillor was the firm favourite. My father was staggered to find the councillor prancing up and down like Jesse Owens in a tiny pair of running shorts, singlet and spiked shoes. What was worse, instead of the hundred yards being paced out very approximately in two-foot strides by one of my father's mates, the councillor, being a councillor, had got a chain measure from the surveyor's department and pegged out a full 100-yards course.

The old man hadn't reckoned for this fastidious approach to what had seemed to him just a simple wager. What's more he felt a bit daft, dressed as he was in ordinary clothes, racing against an opponent who was all kitted out for the Olympic Games. Anyway, he made the best of it. He took his coat and shirt off, tucked his trousers into his socks and put on a pair of old and battered tennis shoes.

By the time he had settled down to his starting position no one gave him much of a chance. He was still a pretty fair athlete and had got ten yards start, but the councillor had impressed everyone by his confident appearance and pre-race limbering-up exercises. It was even suggested that he had been in training for the event.

When they reached the halfway mark the old man was going like a racehorse but was only leading by five yards. But he finally made it, falling across the tape about a yard in front of his opponent. It took him two days off work to recover his wind and a lot longer to collect some of his winnings.

The above is a vivid snapshot of the man who was my father. How much of him I carry with me is probably easier for others to say, as my son Mike will try to do later in the book. I simply adored him. He was generous, loyal and loved his wife and son and grandchildren without reservation and without expecting anything in return. He was the most selfless man I ever met. He was also naturally gregarious, loved meeting new people and found delight in talking the hind legs off them with tall stories told with perfect comic timing and the skill of a snake-oil salesman. When he finally walked away he left his new best friend feeling that they had just been run over by a raconteuring human tsunami.

But if there is one overriding memory of my father it is his hands – rough palms like sandpaper, strong fingers, a miner's hands. When, as a child, he took my hand I felt safer than ever before or since. In many ways I wish I was more like him. I have a tendency to fret, I can be taciturn, I have a short fuse. I am not full of optimism and vim in the face of adversity. But there is within me, like the blue mining scars he carried on his body, an indelible mark that comes from him and I like to think it is the best part of me.

I am drawn to people like my father. We're all drawn to people who help fill in the bits of us that aren't there. That's why I love funny people, love people who can light up a room. It's probably why I so enjoyed being a talk-show host and it's definitely why I fell in love with a beautiful, red-headed young woman on the top deck of a bus in Doncaster. Her relationship with my father was special – they were peas from the same pod. I've been married to her for over sixty years and she's given me three sons of whom I'm proud but not as proud as their grandfather was of them. Which is a perfect moment to once more hand over to my son Mike, who will in the next two chapters explain how John William was far more than just a loving and memorable father, but was also the perfect grandad and the ideal father-in-law.

CHAPTER 5

JOHN WILLIAM PARKINSON, MY GRANDFATHER

'There is an automatic link between the very young and the very old . . . because they are nearer the mysteries of birth and death than the people in the middle who make all the mistakes and are the cause of all the trouble we're in.'

Peter Ustinov on *Parkinson*, 1980

My grandfather with his first grandchild, Andrew: the beginning of his project codenamed 'Yorkshire Grit'.

IT WOULD HAVE BEEN EASY to write a book which lightly skimmed over the surface of my grandfather's life and relationship with his son and to recount the many ways he was a shining beacon of fun and laughter in all our lives, but although that is mostly true, it is also a dishonest way to celebrate the man. Not because beneath the tales my dad recounted and the ones I will share there lurked a dark side to my grandfather. Far from it: no one in the close and extended family I have spoken to has had a bad word to say about him and all have independently agreed that he was simply 'a good man'. (He was obviously much more than that, not least because of the way he transcended his upbringing and job, but it's not a bad epitaph and I know he would have liked it.) It is more that because he was the sun that our little family of planets orbited around, his warm and nurturing light revealed the crags and crevices that our interactions with each other have caused on all our surfaces. For that reason it is necessary to delve a little deeper and explore some uncomfortable and perhaps upsetting observations about how we as a clan have interacted and the sometimes unwitting ameliorating role my grandfather played in all of it.

John William Parkinson took to being a grandfather like a duck to water. In his mind my dad had not produced three sons but three grandsons for him to continue the project codenamed 'Yorkshire Grit' – his search for the saviour of White Rose cricket. I'm sure that at times this made his son feel like he had been merely an audition for the main event. Here my dad recalls when he realised that his father had moved on to the next generation.

The kids came back from two weeks' holiday with their grandparents. They said they had a smashing time. I asked them what they did. 'Played cricket,' they said. I pointed out there must have been occasions in that fortnight when they did something else.

Certainly, they said. For instance, every day they spent a little time in the dining-room and every night they went to bed, but otherwise they played cricket.

Being well acquainted with their grandfather (he doubles as my old man) I could only believe them.

It was he after all who once bowled unchanged into a Force 9 gale on Bridlington beach in 1949 to defeat the residents of a boarding-house called Peaceholme, who had the temerity to challenge our boarding-house to a game of cricket.

His fanaticism on a day so bad that even the seagulls stayed indoors led to mother spending the rest of the holiday in bed with a severe chill after being forced to stand behind the wicket for three hours while father bowled big in-dippers with a dog-eared tennis ball.

That was a long time ago and times change, but not my old man. He could organise a cricket match on an Icelandic trawler given half a chance.

I was intrigued to see what two weeks of being exposed to his idea of a holiday had done to my children, so I invited them onto our lawn, which is thinly disguised as a cricket pitch. Being the senior pro, I batted first and gave the honour of bowling at me to my eight-year-old, Nicholas.

'Scatter wide,' I said to the other two. 'I'm about to give your brother some big stick.'

It must be explained that I fancy my chances against eight-year-old bowlers and Nicholas was no exception. The first thing I noticed was that he had changed his run-up. Instead of his hesitant approach like a man in bare feet treading on tin tacks, he flowed to the wicket. The left shoulder pointed at me, the arm floated the ball down the pitch in a seductive arc. I played forward, getting my eye in prior to belting him out of sight. The ball pitched, turned, came inside the bat and hit me on the kneecap. Through watery eyes I peered down the track. 'And what, pray, was that?' I asked.

'A leg-break,' he said.

'Listen, child,' I said. 'I have played cricket for an eternity and in that time have met only a handful of people who could spin a ball from leg. Among that handful there was not one eight-year-old. Leg-spin bowling is an art to be learned over the years. Now, put all such fancies out of your tiny mind and bowl to me again. We will be kind and say that last ball hit a bump.'

He looked at his elder brother, who was grinning like a goon, and prepared to bowl. Again I played forward and again the ball turned inside the bat and hit my knee-cap. My bump-on-the-pitch theory was looking distinctly threadbare.

'What happened?' I asked.

'I bowled another leg-break,' said Nicholas.

'Show me,' I said. So he tossed up another ball and it turned about six inches. 'How?' I said.

'Grandad taught me. I took six wickets in one match,' he told me.

'I can believe it, for there aren't many eight-year-old leg-spinners around,' I said.

He showed me his grip. The ball looked like a twelve-pound shot in his matchstick fingers. 'I can't spin it properly, so I roll my wrist,' he said.

'Is it difficult?' I asked.

'It's not half so tiring as bowling fast,' he said.

That wasn't my only surprise that day. Having had my nose rubbed in it by my eight-year-old, I decided to take it out on my twelve-year-old. He was always a sucker to the ball on or around his off stump and moving away. He played it with the feet rooted and the bat away from the body. I gave it him first bowl and the result was that our cat patrolling at extra cover nearly lost one of his lives. I tried again and once more his leg thrust across to the pitch of the ball, the bat flashed down and the cat shot up a tree.

'Grandad?' I queried. He nodded. There are times as a parent when you get the feeling that your children are overtaking you and passing you by. I had such a feeling on the day my eight-year-old bowled leg-breaks and my twelve-year-old started playing through the covers like Barry Richards.

Lurking in the background is an elderly man whose only interest in life is teaching his grandchildren how to play the greatest of games. They say you learn from your children and I'm beginning to wise up to that fact.

For instance, next year when they go away for yet another cricketing holiday with my old man I'm not going to waste my time thinking how nice it is to be without them for a while as I did this year. Not me.

Next time I'm taking a refresher course on how to play leg-spin in order that this season's wonder boy will be next season's cannon fodder.

This beautifully rendered moment was so quintessentially English, so overflowing with implicit themes of generational love and the passage of time, that the director John Boorman asked my dad if he could use it as the basis of a scene in his nostalgic semi-autobiographical film *Hope and Glory*. To be fair, there are a few other scenes featuring my grandfather that would have inspired other film-makers of note, mainly, it has to be said, Charles Chaplin.

As far as I remember, it is not true that all we did for two weeks at a holiday camp in Cornwall a few years later was play cricket. In the dry heat of that memorable summer of 1976 we also entered every single sporting competition possible, some of which we'd never played before. Grandad and eldest brother Andrew locked horns in the final of the crazy golf competition, with Andrew claiming to this day he was cheated out of it because his grandad was in charge of both scorecards. We were narrowly beaten in the final of the water polo by a tall athletic family of Swedish extraction, despite the fact that Grandad claimed he couldn't swim so that we played the entire match in the shallow end.

He was, in case you're wondering, an inveterate and outrageous cheat at any game, which meant that he was also the undefeated holiday camp dominoes champion while we were there. There were other notable triumphs in tennis, foot races and football, where middle brother Nicholas revelled in a midfield-enforcer role that, despite being only twelve, meant that grown men entered his part of the pitch with a certain degree of trepidation. Then, of course, there was the inevitable game of cricket against our neighbouring chalet, who – yes, you've guessed it – were a family from Lancashire. Grandad probably put the proviso of a family

The Family Parkinson. Top row, left to right: Mum, Grandad,
Auntie Madge, Gran. Bottom row: Me, Uncle Jim, Nick and Andy.
Dad was undertaking photography duties.
Nick seems unimpressed.

from the Red Rose County as next-door neighbours on his
booking form.

If I'm honest, in these sporting triumphs and near misses I
was the weak link. I remember once being reprimanded by

my captain for abandoning my post at deep square leg so I could emulate my hero the Lone Ranger by hitching a ride on the back of the holiday park owner's colossal Great Dane, who lumbered around the place like a creature from the Jurassic Era. In any case, it was here I discovered that my leanings in the competitive arena were more towards the performing arts. This led me to be top of the holiday camp hit parade for a rendition of a song from the musical *Annie Get Your Gun* which mercifully I have forgotten, though sadly I do still remember it being performed with such precocity that it would have made a young Shirley Temple's toes curl.

In fact, I was robbed in the fancy-dress competition by a girl dressed as Shirley Temple, which I felt contravened the rules as she was already a young girl with curly blonde hair, and simply wearing a dress and singing 'On the Good Ship Lollipop' does not a fancy-dress entry make. By rights, she should have been entered in the lookalike competition, which was won by a man from Glasgow who was the spitting image of Charles Aznavour. And, yes, it's an event that still grates with me today.

My brothers reacted to my elevation to minor-celebrity status with a predictable mixture of embarrassment and the occasional clip round the ear when Gran wasn't looking. My grandad was a little bemused at his youngest grandchild's antics but was happy that I was adding to the family collection of diecast medals and trophies that would require the hiring of a local sherpa to get back home.

That holiday was when we saw our grandad in excelsis. He was in his element. He should have been a redcoat, not a miner. He went round with a smile on his face accompanied by his ancient primus stove, which he took everywhere with him, and despite the holiday camp having a very passable dining hall, he insisted on cooking at least one of our meals on it. This primus stove was so dented it looked like it had seen action in the trenches of the Great War. It was so rickety that it invariably tipped whatever it was cooking onto the grass, and because our chef operated a waste-not-want-not approach, he would simply scoop it back into the pan, insisting, 'A little dirt never did you any harm,' which meant that as a family we followed a raw-food diet way before it became fashionable. It had also, it seems, during its time at the Western Front, been employed as a flame-thrower, because it only had two settings, 'off' and 'blowtorch'. More than once an eyebrow was lost and on several occasions Grandad nearly started bush fires in some of England's most treasured beauty spots.

* * *

Being the youngest grandson, I am in terms of emotional connection the most distant of all the family from my grandfather. He died when I was nine and for the last couple of years of his life he was an ill man who was frustrated at not being the force of nature he had been all his life and not being able to be a proper part of ours. In that sense, his influence on me was reduced. But he did leave his mark. I remember the day he died.

As a child you are sensitive to changes in the rhythms of life, acutely aware of atmospheres, so that even if you don't understand the raised voices or the urgent hushed conversations of adults, the hurried moving to and fro, you know something is wrong. So it was on the morning after the night my grandfather slipped peacefully away.

I was sharing a room with my brother Nick and I remember Mum coming in and telling us that grandfather had 'gone' and that we should stay in our room. Still today I have a somewhat literal mind and can have difficulty decoding the euphemisms employed by people to express unpleasant or sensitive matters, which is probably why I found Les Dawson's old-woman character discussing 'female matters' over the garden wall so hilarious. In the time it had taken me to realise that my grandfather had died, Nick, the rebellious anti-authoritarian and at that stage proto-punk rocker of the three Parkinson boys, had crept out of the door and, for the first time, seen his dad in tears.

At the insistence of my grandmother, and I'm sure for very good reasons, the three boys did not go to the funeral. For me, this was not an issue. As Ustinov says, I was so far away from the mystery of death that it was an incomprehensible event to me. But for my older brothers, it is something that upsets them to this day, particularly the eldest, Andrew. I know this because I spoke to both of them about him, aware that their respective ages at the time of his death of twelve and fifteen make their recollections of our grandad more pertinent and reliable than mine.

We each have our special memories of him. Andrew, the gilded athlete, remembers the time Grandad took him to the local athletics track to practise his 200 metres in preparation for the local district championships. At the time the world record stood at 19.83, set by Tommie Smith and his black leather glove at the 1968 Mexico Olympics, and Grandad was insistent that he would like to see if his eldest grandson had what it took to, if not conquer the world, at least have a chance of being the Yorkshire champion. He told Andrew to get to his marks and he would time this potentially life-changing race on his wristwatch. Andrew duly set off on the 'G' of Go and began his race of destiny.

As he reached the apex of the bend Andrew was slightly perturbed to see out of the corner of his eye that his grandfather and erstwhile coach had struck up a conversation with a man who was attempting to explain to his own young charge the intricate technique of the Fosbury flop, but he continued on and breasted the tape in full *Chariots of Fire* fashion. Then he turned, flushed, exhilarated and keen to learn if he could at last replace double physics with a life in sport.

He discovered that his grandfather was now in the process of marking out a new run-up and take-off point for the high-jump student, as if he had spent every day of his youth in Barnsley curling his body over a bar into a sandpit. When Andrew asked if he had remembered to time the run, our grandfather, who was never lost for words even when caught red-handed, with a quick look at his watch told his eldest grandson that he had just smashed the world record with a time of 18.5 seconds, but given that the track was downhill with the wind behind and he hadn't wound his watch up this morning, this would have to be rounded up to 21.5 seconds, which still today is a world record for a thirteen-year-old.

The middle brother, Nick, remembers our mum having to step in when Grandad's idea of a party game at Nick's eighth birthday was in danger of sending some of the partygoers to childhood-trauma therapists. Grandad had decided to pep up the usual round of pass-the-parcel, pin-the-tail-on-the-donkey, who-feels-the-most-sick-on-cake-and-crisps and who-is-the-first-to-burst-into-tears with a once-in-a-lifetime visit to the Mummy's Cave. This involved each child entering a dark room where the Mummy, aka Grandad wrapped in a bed sheet, was sleeping. The task was to tickle the Mummy's feet and escape before he caught you.

What these poor unsuspecting children were not to know was that inside this genial, mild-mannered man lay a world of mischief and a competitive spirit strong enough to power the National Grid. In other words, there was no way these kids were going to get away with their feet-tickling expedition. Which meant that every time a child came near him he would, Boris Karloff-like, rise up with a bloodcurdling groan of the undead and, as the child turned to escape, hit them on the bottom with a rolled-up newspaper. He was having a whale of a time. The kids, however, were not and my mum had to suggest that it was time to bring the curtain down on his days as a classic horror film actor.

*　　*　　*

I remember a game of cricket on the beach at Hunstanton, where Grandad's best friend and brother-in-law Jim, married to our grandmother's half-sister Madge, had gone to retire after a successful career in engineering. Uncle Jim, as we called him, was a lovely man and a perfect foil to his best mate. He was Stan to Grandad's Ollie, Ernie to his Eric. Jim was quietly spoken, shy and, as you will see, rather accident-prone.

In the company of Grandad, we could never go anywhere and just sit and pass the time. For Grandad a beauty spot was a sports field in nicer surroundings and no journey was complete without an arsenal of sporting equipment. On this particular occasion we decided, well actually he decided, that we were going to play cricket on the beach near Uncle Jim's home. He was bowling, Andrew was batting, Auntie Madge was first slip. Gran at this stage had retired from wicketkeeping and so was in charge of the tea. Nick and I had been dispatched to the edge of the ebbing tide because Grandad had a theory that Andrew was too fond of the sweep shot, a shot Grandad deplored, and an early dismissal might dissuade him from employing it in a real game. Uncle Jim, not being the most lithe of men, reluctantly filled the sizeable hole left by our retired wicketkeeper.

The first ball passed without incident except for a

reminder from my captain that I should stop looking at seagulls and concentrate on the game. The next went down in Parkinson folklore. My grandfather, if he was still around, would claim that it was a perfect unplayable in-swinging delivery of the like not seen since Trueman was putting India to the sword in the 1959 series. The truth is, as my father remembered from his beach-cricket days, he had ensured that the meteorological conditions were in his favour and he was bowling with a tennis ball recently mangled by a local dog, with the aid of a howling cross wind.

The ball started three feet outside off stump and the wind meant that by the time Uncle Jim tried to intercept the ball it was four feet wide of the leg stump and looking likely to go for four byes. Keen to keep his end up and not let the side down, Uncle Jim leapt manfully if not agilely for the ball, missed and fell to earth with a resounding thump, accompanied by a loud tearing noise of the type made when a seam under intolerable strain has finally given out. The seam in question was the one that was holding the seat of Uncle Jim's trousers together. It was not the first time in Parkinson cricketing history that laughter stopped play, but it was the only time that I thought that my grandfather might pass away in a fit of mirth.

*　　*　　*

Grandad was much more than just a chaotic bundle of mischief, however. As my dad says, he was caring and supportive to others and not just his family. He was a neat and orderly man who took pride in his appearance and everything he turned his hand to, even if sometimes, particularly in the DIY arena, it wasn't always an unmitigated success. I still remember the shed he built in the garden of the cottage among the Chiltern Hills that Gran and he retired to. The outside was unpromising, in fact it looked as if a soft breeze might turn it to kindling, but the inside was a cool, dark, orderly sanctuary of recently cleaned and oiled tools and drawers full of impossibly neat boxes of screws and nails, bits of twine and anything else that would allow him to keep his beloved allotment the pride of the parish.

He was, for all that I have written above, a difficult man to lose from your life. For Nick and me he was and always will be a beloved and much-missed grandfather, but for Andrew it was much deeper and it was therefore particularly hard for him to come to terms with not being allowed to say goodbye to the man at his funeral. He had not just lost a grandfather, he had lost his surrogate father.

For reasons I will try to explain later in the book, my dad was not always an easy man to be a son to. This is not to say he was cruel or uncaring, quite the opposite; he was just, as a dad, difficult to get close to, and at times he behaved as if he was not completely comfortable in his own skin, which made intimacy difficult. This was particularly acute in the early relationship between Andrew and Dad.

To be fair, there were good reasons, apart from those that can be traced to their inherently different natures, why they were not as close in the early years as both parties wanted to be. Dad was at the 'T minus 10 seconds' part of his career, a young journalist trying to earn his spurs, driven by that nagging fear of being tapped on the shoulder one day and told to go back to where you came from that all working-class lads and lasses of my father's generation felt when they first stormed the gates of the citadel. This left little time for family life. Plus Andrew was the first child, and as they say, the first child is the one where parents learn to be parents. When I came along, like most youngest children, I had a far easier time in terms of discipline and expectations, with the added support of two big brothers.

Whatever the reasons, Andrew was lucky in that his perceived absence of a dad in his life was filled by Grandad. For Andrew, his grandfather did all the things he wanted his dad to do. He watched him play sport, cajoled and coached him, put literal and figurative plasters on the cuts, and on top of that he acted as a bulwark against a fractious relationship with his dad that stemmed from both parties looking for something in the other that wasn't there.

Andrew adored his grandfather because in the final analysis he is the most like him of anyone in the family. He shares his natural sporting talent, the easy charisma that ensures universal popularity, the gift of optimism in the face of adversity (which is why he has remained a lifelong Leeds United supporter) and the enviable quality of being generally content with his lot in life without the need for the driving, slightly neurotic ambition that was encouraged in my dad by his mother.

She, much more than Grandad, was the real influence that shaped my dad. His relationship with Andrew and to an extent with all his children was coloured by his childhood dominated by a strong, stern and sometimes unforgiving mother. In many ways in the story of our family, the intergenerational relationships do not stem from John William but from Freda Rose and her deep and at times almost suffocating love for her son.

My gran was a difficult soul. She could be argumentative, stubborn and difficult to please, which made her fight against the onset of vascular dementia a thing to behold. She was in no way going to 'go gentle into that good night'. I

Gran with her three grandsons. Eldest brother Andrew
still regrets his choice of hat to this day.

know my brothers felt the rough edge of her tongue as children and struggled to mourn her in the way they did our grandfather, but I had a closer relationship with her, or as close as you could get to her, and it strikes me that it was because there were many aspects of me that reminded her of my dad. I was an introverted, shy, bookish child and I spent more time with her than I did with my grandfather, who I often felt wasn't entirely sure how to deal with his youngest grandchild, particularly as my concerns were not always to do with whether I was gripping the bat correctly or keeping my elbow high in a cover drive.

For that reason, I am able to be more balanced about Gran and the role she has played in all our lives. For all her sharp edges, she was a remarkable woman. Those facets of her personality that in later life were perceived as curmudgeonly were a strong positive force for change in her early life and in the lives of the two men she loved the most. Her inability to accept the status quo and need to kick against convention meant that she drove my dad and my grandad to achieve far more than either had reason to expect.

Not that she had to live vicariously through others. She was bright and talented in her own right. My dad often recalls how, after her death, whilst going through the contents of her cottage in Watlington, he discovered a cache of Patons & Baldwins knitting magazines, with stars such as Paul McCartney and Roger Moore modelling *her* designs. He realised that he had as a child sat for many hours in the cinema or at home whilst his mother knitted, but he and no one else had known quite how good she was.

Yet despite encouraging others to make the best of what they've got, throughout her life she remained reticent about revealing her talent. My mum, when she was presenting the magazine programme *Good Afternoon* in the 1970s,

151

remembers trying unsuccessfully to get my gran to come on the show and contribute to an item about knitting, which was having a resurgence in popularity. This personality kink, combined with the lack of real opportunities for women of her generation, meant she needed others to satisfy the yearning for something better, to take her away from where she felt she never properly belonged, and she was determined that the men in her life would do just that. In doing so she pulled one man from the darkness and sent the other on his way to the stars.

But she was also determined to enjoy the fruits of her labour and proceeded to join my father on that journey and ensure she was front and centre in everything he did. Which of course meant that any woman my father chose to marry would have to get round her first. He chose my mum and an immovable object met an irresistible force.

CHAPTER 6

MARY AGNES HENEGHAN, AKA MUM

And say to mothers what a holy charge
Is theirs – with what a kingly power their love
Might rule the fountains of the new-born mind.

L.H. Sigourney, 'The Mother of Washington

Mary Agnes Heneghan with a very lucky man.

WHILST I MOSTLY AGREE WITH Christopher Hitchens when he said, 'Everyone has a book inside them, which is exactly where I think it should, in most cases, remain,' this is not true of my mum. For my dad, who knows more about her than most, it's a Catherine Cookson story, but only if she was writing it in a really bad mood. He also believes that a film of that book could only do it justice if it was adapted and directed by the Martin Scorsese of *Taxi Driver* vintage.

The issue with getting next summer's blockbuster to the printers is that my mum is reluctant to tell stories about her childhood. What she does reveal is tantalising but disjointed and it is hard to connect the dots in terms of events, narrative and veracity. It's understandable. She has, like many who have suffered trauma in childhood, suppressed, adapted and reimagined her memories so that they can be carried carefully through their life like an unexploded bomb ready at any moment to detonate and unravel them as a person.

What can be discerned is that she was born in South Hiendley, Wakefield. Her mother, Kathleen Heneghan (née Henry), came from South Yorkshire mining stock and, whilst her male relatives would go on to become prominent local politicians, Kathleen entered service as a child, rising from a scullery maid to a cook. She met Thomas Heneghan, an Irish immigrant from a family of farmers in Sligo, who as the youngest son had no stake in the family farm and had to come to England to find work. Like many of his country-men, there was little option for this staunch Irish Catholic, Gaelic-speaking, 6 ft 4 in, broad-shouldered young man but to become a miner, a job that this 'son of the soil' was neither physically nor mentally suited to.

After three male children had died in childbirth they produced Honora, my mum's eldest sister. Meanwhile her father decided he had had enough of toiling underground and, in a dramatic and still to this day somewhat mysterious move, followed the well-trodden route of the Irish diaspora to America, where he found a job more suited to his physique and temperament as a policeman in Chicago. There was a plan that his wife and child would follow, but instead, and again for reasons still unclear to this day, he returned home to work once more in the mines and my mum and another child, Kate, were born.

In contrast to her sisters, who were petite and blonde like their mother, Mary Agnes was the spitting image of her father. She was tall, bonny, athletic and red-haired and her father revelled in this tomboy of a daughter and she loved him in turn. She fondly remembers his strong love of the land, which meant that every spare scrap of garden was turned over to potatoes, rhubarb and other earthly delights, much to the disappointment of his wife, who would have preferred a lawn, whilst at the same time keeping chickens, which for special occasions he slaughtered, to my mum's horror, with the practised skill of a farmer's son.

Her mother in turn, with echoes of my paternal grand-mother, was more concerned with the fact that my mum was obviously bright. She was determined that her middle child should do more with her life than make someone else's life easier. Kathleen had inherited her family's political sensibilities and strongly believed that all her children should expect more from their lives than she had been forced to accept. As a physical embodiment of her overriding belief that what was 'sauce for goose was sauce for the gander', she filled her house with substantial pieces of dark wood furniture which had formerly seen service in the great house where she worked. Her daughters were given elocution lessons and learnt a musical instrument.

It was a household dominated by the Catholic faith, from the religious iconography on the walls to the nightly prayers in front of the fire. Indeed, it is easy to forget how they as a family must have stood out in an Anglican and Nonconformist-dominated mining village. Purely being a 'left footer' was enough to single you out for special treatment, to be forced to live your life as a distrusted outsider, but if your father was also Irish, in an era when the Easter Rising and the Irish Civil War was still fresh in the memory and the issue of Home Rule excited strong and sometimes violent emotions, it would ensure that, as my mother understatedly says, her childhood was 'turbulent'.

It was also tragic. After having earlier lost three sons, Kathleen and Thomas gave birth to Michael John and it was inevitable that after all that loss he would become the apple of his father's eye. My mother was seven when she was present at the time her young brother was run down and killed by the local doctor, who was drunk, and the class system ensured he got off with a slap on the wrist. I say she was present; in fact, she was holding his hand waiting to cross the road with him when he broke from her grasp and she witnessed the whole tragic, horrific incident and carries the irrational guilt for his death with her to this day.

Her father was then terribly injured in the mine, but was refused compensation and came home from an extended stay in hospital broken, diminished and bed-ridden. He never recovered and he died when my mum was ten. Her mother followed a few years later and my mum was parcelled off to relatives on the day of her mother's funeral, after the dividing out of her mum's meagre possessions. But she was not defenceless, despite what her Irish Catholic God had rewarded her faith with. Her mother's desire that she should use her brain had paid dividends.

She had gained a scholarship to a convent grammar school and the next few years was a flurry of running to catch the Flying Scotsman to Leeds for school, overcoming feelings of inadequacy compared to her more privileged classmates, who had the right uniform and the polished accents, whilst doing well enough to gain a place at teacher-training college. This was where the Church repaid her faith and service in full when the Christian Brothers stepped in at my mother's request to convince her family that she should be allowed to continue her studies and not have to leave so she could contribute to the family coffers.

She duly emerged from her time at college a young, forth-right woman unwilling to take a backward step but certainly unprepared to meet a young journalist on a bus in Doncaster.

She had lost one Michael and found another. It's remarkable to think how all of this book is a product of a chance meeting between two strangers. It is sometimes hard to completely erase that sense of a divinity in some form playing a role in all our lives.

The beginning of sixty years together.

As a mum, she has wrapped us in love, at times overprotected us; she has smothered us with care, as people do who come from a fractured or troubled background; she has driven us mad with her bouts of hypochondria; she has right royally stuffed us on the golf course – all while forging a career as a successful broadcaster in her own right, becoming an on-screen confidante, trusted voice and fashion icon for housewives everywhere. In her spare time, she danced with Prince Charles, was compared to Katharine Hepburn by none other than Sidney Poitier and nearly throttled my father when he politely declined Clint Eastwood's offer to join him at Ronnie Scott's jazz club for supper after his appearance on *Parkinson*.

She is full of Celtic eccentricity, gloom and humour, allied to a sense of self that once saw her deck a notoriously 'friendly' fellow golf club member who had the temerity to pat her behind. She's a survivor, but like all survivors is marked and scarred by her early life, which makes her vulnerable and easily undermined. When she met my father she was a woman in her early twenties who had basically raised herself, an orphan with no real support network to turn to. He became her world and his family became the only one she would know. However, little did she realise she was walking into a tight domestic arrangement run by a formidable matriarch, in a hitherto unassailable position, who wasn't prepared to step aside or compromise on the role she occupied in her son's life.

Being one of three siblings means that you share the episodes of your parents' ire and praise, which ensures no one feels too treasured or too criticised and more importantly you can circle the wagons when the parentals get too much. For a parent, it also ensures that you are too busy to become fixated, for bad or good reasons, on one child. I therefore find it hard to imagine the experience of being an only child. My father was not just the apple of his mother's eye but the object of a love bordering on the possessive. Unlike my grandfather, my gran never seemed to totally move on emotionally from her son. He remained the centre of her universe and consequently the rest of us were sometimes made to feel that we were merely people who were lucky enough to be towed along, as indeed she was, in his slipstream.

The result of this, sadly, was that she became something of a divisive force in the family, which put her at odds with my mum and my brothers but not me because, as I have already said, I think she could see her son in me and in many ways tried to shape me as she had shaped him. Interestingly, given what my dad has revealed about her early life and the forced role she had in helping send her brother to Oxford, I

Gran: the engine of Dad's ambition.

remember on several occasions my gran taking me on trips to Oxford to look around the colleges. She was showing me where she thought I should aim for and, despite missing the mark, looking back I can see what a force of nature she would be if she believed in you.

In the face of all this, my grandfather seemed largely powerless. His staunch defending of his grandsons against the occasional outbursts of paternal advice which in tone and delivery would have been welcomed in the living rooms of Victorian Britain was missing when it came to his wife.

163

His love for her and the power in her that had transformed his life made him, if not compliant, then unable to smooth the edges of her ultimately self-destructive behaviour. Her son was equally transfixed by this woman who had been the centre of his whole world, had made him see the possibilities of life beyond the pit village and yet would not let him go, set him free to properly share himself with others. My eldest brothers drew together. I was mostly buried in a book, but my mum was left exposed and, because of the fragility of her self-confidence caused by her upbringing, was unable to place a flag in this new territory with any sense of permanence.

What my mother did have, though, was the devotion of her father-in-law who, from the first time he met her, adored this girl 'our Michael' had found. She drew much that had been missing in her early life from him and in turn he drew much from her. He stood in for the father she had lost too early in her life and she gave him the female warmth that was at times lacking in his marriage because of the way his son Michael dominated the emotional landscape of his wife. They were, as my father says, 'peas from the same pod'.

Their relationship was landmarked by various adventures, mainly in DIY and gardening, which usually resulted in my mum having to tell him to stop before any further damage was caused and a man subsequently having to be employed to make good the work. They also went on Don Quixote-like expeditions, despite neither of them having a sense of direction, with the result that a journey of thirty minutes became one of many hours lost down the leafy byways of England. One story will suffice to sum up their closeness and their shared capacity for madcap adventures instigated by my grandfather, with my mother the not always willing conspirator.

My mother had been married a year and was nervously awaiting the birth of her first child, whom she would christen, to keep her Irish Catholic God happy, Andrew John Parkinson. She was living in Manchester, my father was working in London on the *Daily Express* and the National Health Service awaited the first pangs of labour. But my grandfather had other ideas, as my father remembers:

When Andrew was about to be born I was living in Manchester but working in London. I had reached a perfectly normal and satisfactory arrangement with the welfare state whereby my firstborn would be delivered into the world in a Lancashire hospital. Near the expected date of the birth I received a phone call from my father.

'Well, it's done then,' he said.

'What is?' I asked.

'I've moved t'wife to a nursing home in Yorkshire,' he said.

'But why? Mary was perfectly happy in Manchester,' I said.

'Maybe, but we've not only her to think about. What about t'baby?' he said.

'What difference does that make?' I asked.

There was a long pause. He was obviously trying hard to control himself. 'Supposin' it's a boy,' he said.

'I very much hope it is,' I said.

'And if it's born in Lancashire, what happens then?' he said.

'Tell me,' I said.

'It can't play for Yorkshire at cricket, that's what!' he yelled, his temper getting the better of him. 'Anyway, like I've told you, I've had them shifted. It's proper thing to do, lad.'

A month later my first child, a boy, was born in a Wakefield nursing home. His name is Andrew. He was a good cricketer but he didn't play for Yorkshire. 'Point is he *could* have if he wanted to,' said my father. And he died a happy man.

To any ambitious film-makers seeing an opportunity, it's too late: we've secured the film rights to my mother's life story and that is the opening scene.

My grandfather was a source of joy and solace to us all – not just to his son. He deserves this tribute, but as my dad will now explain, it was difficult to find the right way to do his and our family story justice until we stumbled across an unusual resource that helped to show us the way forward.

CHAPTER 7

TELL ME ABOUT YOUR FATHER

They fuck you up, your mum and dad.
   They may not mean to, but they do.
They fill you with the faults they had
   And add some extra, just for you.

Man hands on misery to man.
   It deepens like a coastal shelf.
Get out as early as you can,
   And don't have any kids yourself.

Philip Larkin, 'This Be the Verse'

WHILST AN APPEARANCE ON PIERS Morgan's show
provided the inspiration, the shape and content of this
journey to the heart of the man I most looked up to was not
immediately clear. As with all great expeditions, it does help
to have an inkling of where you are heading. Which is where
another unlikely source of inspiration reared its head, in the
form of Rob Brydon, and turned this book into far more
than a mere collection of misty-eyed reminiscences.

I bow the knee to no one in my admiration for Rob. He is
one of our most talented comedy actors and writers and
when for a short time he was the host of his own talk show,
The Rob Brydon Show, he revealed himself as a not-half-bad
interviewer, despite the majority of the show being played
for laughs. Being a generous soul, at a mellow stage in my
life and career where I feel the urge to mentor and encourage the next generation, I have always given him such positive feedback. The pleasing result is that I have become

friends with this genuinely nice man. Which is why I find it so hurtful that he occasionally repays my affection and support with mockery of yours truly.

When he and co-conspirator Steve Coogan embark on another *Trip* abroad I immediately contact my lawyers to alert them to the possibility of slanderous impersonations of me by Mr Brydon. Such is my affection for Rob that I can't help placing the majority of the blame for this juvenile behaviour on Coogan, who to my mind is obviously leading this innocent man from the Valleys astray, but then this might also be influenced by the fact that Mr Coogan comes from the wrong side of the Pennines. However, both of them should be congratulated for repeatedly convincing the powers that be to pay for them to go on an extended holiday to enjoy each other's company and generally show off their talent.

I felt the same kind of professional jealousy when I was younger about my dear departed friend Alan Whicker when he was bestriding the glamorous narrow world like a broadcasting colossus. But then I would witness and wonder at yet another faultless piece to camera – done, as it had to be in those days because of the limits of the technology, in one take without autocue – and realise that I was probably safer in a nice warm studio.

Now, when Rob does his thing I, like all people who are impersonated, can't and don't believe that I sound or behave remotely like the gabbling, twitching, adenoidal, flat northern vowel-spewing monster that he transforms me into. Yet friends and even beloved grandchildren tell me it is very good, particularly, as Mike pointed out, the way he lampoons my style of questioning by occasionally introducing his impersonation with the line 'Tell me about your father'.

As I spend most of the time cringing in discomfort whilst watching Rob impersonating me, I hadn't noticed that he had also occasionally condensed my interview technique into one question, but once I had got over my indignation at this affront to my art by lying down in a darkened room with a poultice over my fevered brow, I realised that this small revelation intrigued me, particularly in light of the task we had set ourselves in this book.

I wondered if it was true. Did I have such a fascination with the father/son relationship that in any interview I attempted, where appropriate, to get others to talk about their father? The simple fact is that anyone interested in doing a biographical interview should obviously look for clues to the wellspring of a person's life choices as an adult in their childhood, to see how the separate forces of mum and dad, whether for good or bad, wrought changes on the child that echoed into their adult life and informed the way they conducted themselves. However, I never thought I fixated particularly upon the male side of this equation.

With the theme of this book firmly in my thoughts, plus the possibility of providing evidence to the aforementioned lawyers to confirm the flagrant inaccuracies of Mr Brydon's lampooning of myself (who, need I remind you, has been referred to as a 'National Treasure'), I set my co-author the task of looking through my old interviews to establish whether the joke contained a grain of truth. The results, it must be said, are fascinating. There is no real evidence of an unhealthy interest in the father/child dynamic on my part, but there are a number of instances where I asked about it and the subsequent answer and discussion yielded profound and at times surprising insights into the unfathomable emotional complexity of this relationship, which proved more than useful when writing this book and reassessing my father. I'll let Mike take you through what we found.

My dad has always been more comfortable writing and wondering about others whilst cloaking his own experiences and emotions within tales of sporting endeavour and other memories laced with humour and a small serving of myth.

It's not that he is uninterested in his inner life, it's just he finds it hard to examine and reveal it. Which is why he is in his particular field a peerless interviewer. He is fascinated by what makes people tick because there is a need in him to make sense of his own internal mechanism. It's introspection disguised as an interview and that's why there are only a select few who can actually do the job well and why his interviews are a rich source of unintentional autobiography and, for the purposes of this book, a vital and fascinating resource.

Throughout most of my time working with my father, the foundation stone has been the *Parkinson* archive. Once he had decided to hang up his interviewing cloak in 2007, we formed a production company with the express intention of bringing all the *Parkinson* shows under one roof and using them as the basis for the production of programmes, books and live projects. Every one of the 600-plus shows both here and in Australia was tracked down and watched and the best and most compelling bits from each programme were noted down. The process took over a year but the result is that not only has 'The *Parkinson* show, 1971 to 2007' become my specialist subject (one that could easily propel me to the *Mastermind* crown, or at least into the lead until the general knowledge round), but we have also created an archive that reveals how the show was so much more than a celebrity gabfest, covering topics and themes that belied the impression created by the walk-down music and the general Saturday-night light-entertainment feel of the programme. For that reason, I was pretty confident I could find what Rob Brydon had been cheekily hinting at.

Taken together, the interviews I unearthed revealed to us that there are myriad ways a father and a child can inter-relate, determined as much by family circumstances as by personality traits, which makes it a game of chance in the way that they will then co-exist. Some are lucky and some less so, but what is fascinating is that although many of the people my father interviewed were at the top of their game, doing the job they loved and leading what seemed to be fulfilled and enviable lives, some were stalked by the spectre of the father figure. There were those who were still struggling to come to terms with this relationship, still licking the wounds and wondering about the real nature of the man who had helped bring them into the world and shaped it for them for the few years they were with him as a child.

As my dad has already said, any interviewer worth their salt will always look for clues about interviewees in their childhood and the relationship with their parents as to how they became, not as the public sees them, but the man or the woman behind the talent and the PR. With **Val Doonican**, it was clear he came from a rumbustious, large family steeped in music but, though it was known that he had lost his father at an early age, there was nothing in the research to indicate that this would be a fecund area for exploration – until quite out of the blue he told this story about him.

MICHAEL: You mentioned he died when you were thirteen?

VAL DOONICAN: I knew nothing. I knew there was something wrong. I never knew what was wrong with him, but I knew there was something because he stopped going to work, and I couldn't understand this at all. I knew things were a bit slack in the job where he worked but I didn't understand why he had his good clothes on during the week and that sort of thing. And he was beginning to look very clean and well shaven, and it wasn't like him: he was always sort of black from the job.

So I remember one day, I shall never forget it actually, he called me down to the hut and I sat down on the step and he said to me, 'I'd like you to do something for me, son, and I don't want you to say anything to your mother.' And, of course, in our house

177

that was impossible. You couldn't do anything without everybody knowing about it. You know, we always said the first up in the morning was the best dressed.

He handed me a 2 lb jam jar and a pair of scissors and he said, 'I want you to go out to Looby Lane.' Now this was a little lane near my house where courting couples used to go, all covered in blackberry briars, which wasn't very good for the courting couples, but he said, 'I want you to go up Looby Lane. The blackberry briars are just coming into bloom and I want you to cut the little blossoms off the end and put them in the jam jar and bring them back to me.' And he said, 'Don't tell your mother about this.' I asked what they were for and he said, 'Shhhh, mum's the word, off you go.' So I went and got these blackberry briars and brought them back to him, waiting to see what happened. He just took them and said, 'Off you go now. Go on, off you go.'

And the next morning, we didn't have a bathroom, you see, and there was a tap on the wall out in the yard and I went out to get some water to wash myself to go to school and my mother said to empty out some rubbish for her. I emptied it into the dustbin and there at the bottom were the blackberry briars, in a little heap, and they were all wet and everything, and I thought, 'Well, there's gratitude for you. He's just thrown them all out.'

Now, about fifteen years after that I was in Scotland. I was touring with Jack Ratcliffe's show and I came back to my digs one night and I was looking through some old books while I was waiting for my beans on toast after the show. I looked at this book and it was called *The Home Physician* and I turned it over and I was absolutely sickened when I saw written down there that it was widely believed in country districts in Ireland many years ago that if you cut the ends off blackberry briars and boiled them and drank the water off them it would cure cancer of the throat.

Well, I nearly died. I was thinking of my poor dad and he was down in his shed all on his own. He had cancer of the throat and he knew he was dying and he didn't want to upset my mum, you know, didn't want to tell her. And the loneliness of the whole thing. I burst out crying when I read it, I couldn't believe it.

MICHAEL: What an amazing story.

VAL DOONICAN: He finally went into hospital and I used to go and see him every day when I'd come home from school. My mother used to get him his tobacco and his matches and the daily paper and everything and I used to take them up to him. As time went on his whole face sort of disappeared, bless him, and he was all in bandages, his whole head was in bandages, and the last thing he said to me – it's got to be the most profound thing I've ever heard in my life.

I sat by the bed talking to him and he said to me, 'You know I'm going to die, don't you?' And I said, 'Yes I do. Mum told me you're going to die.' He said, 'I think I'm going to die pretty quickly, so I would like it if you didn't come and see me any more.' And I said, 'OK,' and I got up to say goodbye to him. Then he said, 'Before you go, there's something I need to say to you. You think I'm terrific, don't you?' And I said, 'Yes I do.' And he said, 'I think before I die it's only fair I should say to you that I'm not. Because when I'm gone I'm sure a lot of people will tell you I am no good, and there's nothing that would please me more than if you say, "Yes I know, he told me that himself."' Isn't that lovely?

Another congenial man beloved of audiences was the agreeable face of Hollywood that was **James Stewart**. He was, as fellow actor Anthony Quayle described him, 'everything the British audience wants an American to be, but so rarely is'. It was clear from the way he talked about his father that Stewart's mild-mannered, laid-back charm, laced with a wicked sense of humour, was an inherited family trait.

JAMES STEWART: My father had a hardware store in Western Pennsylvania, that's in the soft coal area of our country, near the big industrial city of Pittsburgh. His father established the hardware store, and he was able to celebrate the one hundredth anniversary of the hardware store before he died. I think the reason he kept the store for so long was because he was sure that people were going to catch up with me out in Hollywood and I would have something to go back to.

He wasn't too happy about the acting profession as a way to make a living. When I came back and announced that I wasn't going to go to graduate school and learn to be an architect – I was going to Broadway and have a small part in a play – he just reached for a chair and sat down, but bless their hearts, both my mother and my father said, 'OK.' But my father had the final say. When I was leaving to

181

seek my fortune on the stage, he said, 'Well, I expect this is fine.' He said, 'There haven't been any Stewarts in show business except one, a third cousin of yours, Ezra, and he ran away and joined the circus, and he's the only Stewart that I know of that's ever been to jail, but good luck to you.'

But it turns out that Stewart Senior was as proud as punch of his son's achievements. He may never have told him so to his face, but indirectly he gave him the ultimate accolade by putting the Oscar that Stewart won in 1941 for *The Philadelphia Story* in pride of place in the front window of his beloved hardware store.

Now let's move from the sublime to the ridiculous. There was one interview my father did that revealed a father/son remembrance that no one can fully understand unless you were born into the privileged aristocracy of the last century. He interviewed Henry George Alfred Marius Victor Francis Herbert, aka **the 6th Earl of Carnarvon**, or 'Porchie' as he preferred to be known, on two occasions and both were memorable in the sense that it was like watching a walking, talking relic of a time when Britain ruled the waves, the sun never set on our Empire, ladies left when the port arrived and forelocks were tugged with vigour. He was like a character from *Downton Abbey* – indeed, the show is filmed at his erstwhile ancestral home – but only if it had been written by P.G. Wodehouse.

His father, the 5th Earl, was the man who had employed archaeologist Howard Carter to supervise the excavations in Egypt's Valley of the Kings, which resulted in the discovery of Tutankhamun's tomb. It was reputed that the Earl's death shortly after the discovery was due to a curse released when the boy king's tomb was so impudently defiled, but as you will see, such was his treatment of a young Porchie that his death nearly occurred well before the pharaoh got his alleged revenge

MICHAEL: Your father called you Porchie, didn't he?

LORD CARNARVON: No, he called me Porchester.
He was a very tough guy. Of course, things were different in those days. You know: 'Little boys should be seen and not heard.' That was the theme of the whole thing.

MICHAEL: We're now talking about the Edwardian era, aren't we?

LORD CARNARVON: I was born in 1898, and I used to get an awful lot of stick from my parents, which was normal, the ordinary thing. One only saw him rather rarely.

MICHAEL: And you were kept away from the adults?

LORD CARNARVON: Oh, very much! Well, I mean one was kept away from one's family. We used the red stairs – the back stairs – occasionally brought down after lunch, especially if there was a big party, and my father would look at his watch and say, 'Well, children, that's right, now go for a nice long walk.' That was the form.

MICHAEL: So you never grew up in a kind of loving relationship?

LORD CARNARVON: Nothing cosy or loving about it, no. I once went to the length of hiding behind a bush with a stiletto that I'd found somewhere in the house, because my father had beaten me with a home-made birch rod. And beaten me good and proper: bare bum and so on. And I was tied up to a bedpost.

MICHAEL: Really?

LORD CARNARVON: Oh rather! And my tutor had to rub in ointment and he said to me, 'My friend, I think you'll be eating your meals for the next few days standing up.' How right he was!

MICHAEL: You started off that story by saying you took a stiletto?

LORD CARNARVON: Well, I did because at one moment I
had thoughts of being very clever, hiding behind a
bush – I was only about knee-high to a duck – leaping
upon my father, who was athletic and six foot, and
stabbing him. I thought, 'I'll get my own back, I'll be
happy.'

MICHAEL: You actually lived in terror of him, did you?

LORD CARNARVON: I really did, yes. A very sad thing,
really. One wishes one hadn't now, because in later
life, when I got older, I found he was awfully nice in
his own way.

Another who decided attack was the best form of defence
against a brutal father was the late, great **Kirk Douglas**.
Born to a dirt-poor Orthodox Jewish Russian father, he and
his siblings spent most of their lives in fear of this brooding,
menacing presence at the dinner table. In echoes of his most
iconic and memorable role, on one occasion he decided to
stand up for the downtrodden.

KIRK DOUGLAS: My father, by the way, was quite a character. He was a very powerful man, a peasant. He also
drank a lot, and I have often thought that one of the
bravest moments in my life was one day when I stood

up to him. I was about ten years old, and we were all sitting around the table – my six sisters, my mother and I, and my father in one of the rare moments that he was with us. We were drinking tea out of Russian-style glasses. My father was breaking off a piece of sugar and sipping the tea and everybody was frightened of him. He was just overpowering and in a mean mood, and I don't know why, suddenly I took a spoon, filled it with hot tea and flicked it right in his face. Well, I tell you – he grabbed and he threw me. I'm so restrained usually, but that moment is so vivid in my mind. It's almost like an act that I feel saved me, a moment that dared me to do something and I did it. When you're that young, you actually think you're risking your life.

Someone else for whom economics had as much to do with the dysfunction of the relationship as personalities was the former Oasis frontman **Noel Gallagher**. It was an interview that my dad was initially very reluctant to do. Having started his career as a newspaper reporter and cut his teeth in television as a producer, my dad was much more than just the host of the show that bore his name. He had finely honed editorial instincts and he wanted to be sure that each guest his production team suggested passed muster in terms of a story to be told plus the means and willingness to tell it.

All guest suggestions for forthcoming shows were discussed at weekly production meetings, and when I was the producer at ITV these were often occasions for full and frank exchanges, which, it has to be said, were sometimes additionally charged because of our own unique father-and-son dynamic. Getting Noel Gallagher down my dad's stairs was one of the biggest battles we had. My dad was genuinely concerned about whether there was an interviewable man behind the image portrayed in the tabloids, not always unfairly, of a hell-raising, sibling-bashing yobbo. And, of course, in his musical-snob opinion, Noel's and Oasis's music fell some way short of his Hall of Fame entry requirements. But I and the team persevered and I know he was glad we did.

It turned out to be one of his and indeed my favourite interviews during his time at ITV. Noel was a great interviewee, candid, engaging, surprising, interestingly contrary – and another survivor of a brutal upbringing in equally brutal unforgiving times.

MICHAEL: And also there was violence in your family – your father was a violent man.

NOEL GALLAGHER: Well, yeah, saying that, probably not any more than any of my other mates' families on our street.

MICHAEL: But that wouldn't be saying much, would it? Because you grew up in a very tough neighbourhood.

NOEL GALLAGHER: Yeah, but it was the seventies, and this was before the New Age man was the trendy thing to be. It was a violent time, the seventies, do you know what I mean?

MICHAEL: It wasn't just not changing nappies: he used to beat you up, your dad. That's what he used to do, he used to beat you.

NOEL GALLAGHER: Yeah, he did, yeah.

MICHAEL: And you used to lie in bed awake at night thinking, 'Is he going to come in and whack me?'

NOEL GALLAGHER: Yeah.

MICHAEL: And you developed a stammer because of that.

NOEL GALLAGHER: Yeah, how do you know all this?

MICHAEL: And what fascinates me is that people now talk about 'sink estates' and they talk about youth and they talk about the problems they have, but you lived all that, and you lived it at a time when they weren't as concerned as maybe they are now. And what fascinates me is how a kid who has no hope and no future grows up. What was it like?

NOEL GALLAGHER: I don't consider my upbringing to be worse than any other on my street, or any other guys my age that I used to knock around with. But it is kind of soul-destroying, or it was in the eighties, when you're going to sign on with your dad and with your best mate and his dad. And you think, our dads haven't even got a job, so what hope is there for us?

So that in itself breeds frustration, but none of that has ever come out in my music. My music has always been pretty positive, and I've always been kind of fascinated by life. I don't want to sound too weird about it, but every day I would wake up and it was great because something great might happen today, do you know what I mean? I wouldn't wake up in a negative mood any day, and I never do. But those were kind of rough times when there was no work in Manchester, not only for you but for your parents too.

Noel, like Kirk Douglas, had found a way to slay the monster masquerading as his father. Kirk tackled it head on. Noel retreated inward, found release in music and quite remarkably, without any outside help and by his own sheer will and natural intelligence, had seemingly come to terms with and drawn a line under his father's behaviour by rationalising it within the context of the time and place they were living through together – although the ingestion of large quantities of drugs in his earlier years may have gone some way towards dulling any residual pain.

Others my dad interviewed, however, struggled to do the same and, despite seeking answers for most of their adult life, the legacy still troubled them. In fact, 'haunted' would be a better word. One that stood out was the British actor **Robson Green** who, in echoes of my dad's own childhood, was born to a Northumbrian miner, but that is where the similarities end.

MICHAEL: What about your dad, because he figures large in your life, doesn't he? He was a dominant sort of figure.

ROBSON GREEN: Absolutely, and we've only recently resolved it.

MICHAEL: Resolved what?

ROBSON GREEN: Well, we'll go through it, I guess. It's sort of been a therapy during my life. Dad was a miner, as was his dad, and he worked down the mine for thirty-five years. Went down the black hole for thirty-five years of his life. And I don't think he enjoyed the experience because I could tell he had that look in his eye, he didn't enjoy it, and I know he didn't want me to go down there. He found it very difficult to accept that he had no recognition. You know, we don't recognise miners and he found it very difficult to be called 'scum' by our national newspaper. So Dad came from work I think an unhappy man. He didn't enjoy his work and sometimes took that out on his family. And he knows. He said, 'And you're going on *Parkinson* and you can tell him I clouted you.'

MICHAEL: You've cleared this with him, have you? And he did? And was it brutal in that sense?

ROBSON GREEN: No, not brutal, just, you know, I think parents just want their children to be perfect, you know. He hit me in rhythm. You know what I mean? 'What – have – I – told – you?' Do you know what I mean? 'And there's plenty more where that came from.' Which I never understood. And the fact was he was a big guy. When you realise I was aged about seven. He was about eighteen stone. Amazingly big, powerful man. He was the hardest in the street.

MICHAEL: So you must have grown up in fear of him, in a sense?

ROBSON GREEN: Yeah.

MICHAEL: And that lasted until when?

ROBSON GREEN: When Mum and Dad got divorced, most definitely. And you get these intellectuals and these social workers, and I hear them going, 'Oh, divorce, must have a terrible psychological effect on you.' Well, we went, 'YES!!! He's gone!! Fantastic!! Let's party!!' So once he left there was a certain amount of freedom. I chatted with Dad, but I never really saw him again until I did my first professional job in a theatre.

MICHAEL: What was his reaction to you, your ambition to go into the theatre?

ROBSON GREEN: He never knew about it. I kept it from him. Can you imagine – 'Dad, I'm going to be an actor.' 'Don't be so stupid.' I'm not from an acting background. I'm sure he had various images of what acting is about.

MICHAEL: You were reconciled in the end, and what is the relationship now? Obviously a good one, as he said, 'Go on and tell them how brutal I was to you.'

ROBSON GREEN: The relationship is grand. We go to the match every week. He is my finest critic. You know, he watched a show and I have to say it was awful and

I played my part with a confidence that was wholly unwarranted. He rang up and said, 'I hope you weren't paid for that.' But Dad's great and you know recently me and Vanya have had a son, Taylor, and I didn't realise the effect it would have on Mum and Dad, having a son, having a baby.

MICHAEL: A grandson?

ROBSON GREEN: Yes, their grandson. I didn't realise how important it would be to Dad. I remember ringing him from the hospital and going, 'Dad, you have a grandson,' and he choked, I know, but we were up there recently and Dad was holding Taylor and I'm not romanticising the image, but there was Dad holding Taylor, looking at him, and Taylor was smiling and Dad was smiling and I just realised at that moment maybe Dad looked at me like that when I was born.

And I thought, my God, that's it, love is everything, and I said to Dad, 'Is it better to be loved or feared?' And he knows, and he knew what he was doing to us, he knew it was hard.

That wondering about the man who is your father – what motivates him, what emotional life lies within and ultimately how all this comes together in the way he does what he does to you – is a constant theme that emerges in the interviews we have chosen. It was put most eloquently by that epitome of a Hollywood leading man, **Tom Hanks**. Hanks specialises in portraying decent men struggling to maintain their moral and emotional equilibrium against often insurmountable odds. In a real sense, he's the modern-day Jimmy Stewart. Think Captain Miller in *Saving Private Ryan*, Jim Lovell in *Apollo 13* and, even though blissfully unaware of what he was actually living through, Forrest Gump.

In all of his movies his acting is like a still point in the eye of a hurricane. He's like putting on a favourite overcoat on a cold day, and he represents the quiet, unassuming determination and decency we wished we all had ourselves, which is why he is always so watchable and the audience is magnetically drawn towards him. In the interview my dad did with him you realise that this is no coincidence and you quickly discover that his on-screen persona is an extension of the man himself. Beneath that urbane, witty, old-school movie-star patina there lies a humble, thoughtful, emotionally intelligent man who wonders about things beyond the narrow, privileged confines of Hollywood and about how he came to be where he is and why he chose to do the job he did.

He was on the show to promote the film *Road to Perdition*, which in its writing and execution is much more than a simple gangster movie. At its heart it is a study of the relationship between fathers and sons, and the central one between Hanks as Michael Sullivan the mob enforcer and his son, Michael Jr, who has no idea what Daddy does when he goes to the office, is a moving study in the emotionally constipated way fathers and sons often interrelate, despite yearning love on both sides oozing from every pore.

At the end of the film, a grown-up Michael Jr is asked about his feelings for his father, a father he now realises was capable of acts of murderous violence and yet had spent his whole life trying to protect him from the truth in the hope he would choose another path. He simply answers, 'He was my father,' which when you come to think about it is the perfect answer to an almost unanswerable question, but it wouldn't make much of a book. In a similar vein, my dad asked Tom Hanks if the movie had made him think about his own relationship with his father. His answer was both moving and thought-provoking.

TOM HANKS: My father was miraculous with any sort of tool. A shovel, a wrench, a pair of pliers. And I remember watching him. We were very different, the

195

two of us. I was very personable; he was very shy. I was very outgoing; he couldn't be outgoing if he tried. But I remember watching him when he'd be hard at work in the back yard digging or chopping away at something with all the vigour in the world and I was thinking, 'Who is this guy? How did I end up here and do I have anything in common with this man whatsoever?'

And then in the course of growing up, particularly as I got older, we'd find a kind of common language that was not really based on thinking the same things but an understanding of each other that stemmed from a degree of admiration. When I started doing theatre in high school and college he would come and see me in shows and I would ask him, 'Well, what did you think of it, Dad?' and he'd just go [*shakes head*] because he could not understand how a human being could get up and do such things. He's looking at me, thinking, 'Where does he come from, this kid? How does he get up there and do this thing?'

MICHAEL: Was he a hero to you?

TOM HANKS: He was. He was also a burden to me, quite frankly, and I think that's the truth about that line – 'every father is a hero to his son' – I think every father can also be a burden to his son. He at times was an intimidating man simply because he was uncommunicative from the perspective he just didn't know what to say. He didn't know how to tell me what was going on in his life.

The sense of bafflement about how you came to be related when you seemingly have so little in common in terms of how your lives have panned out or how you are as people and the inability to bridge the yawning gulf must echo with many of us – including, it has to be said, myself.

There was, however, one interview we revisited that strongly resonated with us both, and in many ways opened up the way forward, and that was the interview with **Sting**, one of our most gifted and successful songwriters and musicians. He had just performed one of my dad's favourites of his many enigmatic, darkly tinged love songs, 'When We Dance', and then he sat down to talk about his recently released autobiography.

MICHAEL: When I read the book, I kept thinking of a black-and-white movie they must make of it directed by Ken Loach or someone like that. It's got all the kinds of elements you need. It's got this extraordinary moment where you as a child growing up in Wallsend discover that your mum's having an affair, which has this effect which ripples on throughout your life, even to the present time. Just explain the circumstances of what happened.

STING: Well, my mum was this wonderful, beautiful creature, very quixotic and incredibly romantic. Desperately in love with movies and wanting to be loved. She needed affection. My father was very stoic and didn't demonstrate affection very easily. He adored my mother and adored us, but he was one of those people who couldn't really say it. He couldn't really hug you, he couldn't really praise you, so she desperately needed this intimacy, which she had every right to find somewhere else and she did. But I discovered them together, her and her lover, and it obviously had a great, a huge effect on my whole life.

MICHAEL: Absolutely.

STING: Probably my whole creative life too.

MICHAEL: But in the sense that, and you make the point in the book, you sought refuge in music. This angry piano player.

STING: Yes, the song I just sang is from the lover's point of view. I keep changing – I sometimes sing about my dad, sing about my mother, I sometimes sing about her lover. It's an interesting landscape to be a writer in and I'm grateful for it, is what I'm saying.

MICHAEL: Yes, you are the man you are because of that. It's shaped you. It has to get out somehow.

STING: Yes. It's a prerequisite of being artistic, being creative. It's like a pearl. It doesn't happen without a piece of aggravation, a bit of dirt inside the oyster, and you build something up and that becomes your life, and so I'm very grateful for my parents and what they did.

MICHAEL: Your father very much loved your mother and had to live with this betrayal all his life and you must have sided with him?

STING: My dad was this wonderful, heroic man. He was a milkman and every morning, 365 days a year, he'd be out delivering milk in all kinds of weather. A very heroic, stoic man and I adored him. But he couldn't really just be warm, it was very hard for him. Even though I knew he adored me, he couldn't say it and it took me a long time to work that out.

MICHAEL: Did he ever say anything complimentary to you?

199

STING: On his deathbed he did, yes. He was dying for a
few days, and it was the first time I noticed he had the
same gnarly kind of hands as I do. And I said, 'Dad,
we have the same hands,' and he said, 'Aye, son, but
you use yours better than I use mine.' And that broke
me up because that was the first time he had really
paid me a compliment. I mean, what timing he had. It
just made everything worthwhile.

Sting's description of his and his father's hands was the key
that opened the door to this exploration of the father/son
dynamic because it was strikingly similar to how my dad
described his final goodbye to his father. He remembers
being by his bedside as my grandfather lay dying in our
home. Both of them had imbibed enough pain-relieving
medication to allow them to talk freely and openly. It was
then that his father told my dad how proud he was, but
reminded him that whatever he had achieved, it wasn't like
playing for Yorkshire.

During this precious, woozy time together, my dad
remembers looking at his father's hands and ruminating on
the gulf between what he did with his hands and what his
father did with his. My dad was a scribe; his father was a
miner. They had the same hands, shaped by genetics, but

Behind a typewriter, where my dad is happiest.

they had been sculpted by the different forces that had buffeted them throughout their lives.

My dad remembers feeling a terrible sense of guilt and injustice that his father had done what he had had to do all his life only to be laid low when he should have been enjoying his golden years, and thinking how much he had to

201

thank his father for being part of the reason he hadn't had to put his life on the line every day he went to work, monumental drinking bouts in the early days of Fleet Street excepted.

Their hands lay next to each other on top of the blanket and he realised then that it would be a lovely and evocative image if he ever got round to writing the book about his father that had sat on the back burner for so long.

The snippets of interviews featured above, and many others that didn't quite make the cut, have been so useful. They've shown us that we were not ploughing a lonely furrow, that every son, to differing degrees, struggles with the father figure. They have helped my father address his mass of emotions and place them in a semblance of order, and for me they also raised larger, more generic questions about the nature of the father/son relationship and consequently made me reassess my own with my co-author.

CHAPTER 8

LIKE FATHER, LIKE SON — THE NEXT GENERATION

The fault, dear Brutus, is not in our stars,
But in ourselves, that we are underlings.

William Shakespeare, *Julius Caesar*

*The Parkinson boys. I shall never forgive my
mother for dressing me like that!*

AS THAT OSCAR-WINNING SONG CLAIMS, 'Love is a Many-Splendoured Thing', and never more so than when you are trying to summarise the way it manifests itself between fathers and sons and how that inevitably ripples down and through succeeding generations of a family. All that is written here is inspired by and is an attempt to unravel that uniquely human emotion, love. A simple word that can cover a whole gamut of behaviour in humans, ranging from the erotic to the nurturing, from the possessive to the destructive.

It could be argued that it is no surprise that some men, in differing ways and with differing levels of trauma, struggle to understand or be at peace with their fathers. Because of the nine months you spend in intimate union with your mother there is a bond with her that exists before birth that, all things being equal, transcends all normal rules of love. On a visceral, subconscious level you have absorbed a piece of each other. Yet, despite carrying the genetic imprint of your father, you are unknown to him and he to you until the moment of birth.

You are then born to a man that you didn't choose at a stage in their life you also didn't choose, which for good and bad reasons could affect their behaviour towards you, and yet you are hardwired to love him and to look to him for warmth and guidance, which is in no way guaranteed to be reciprocated in the manner you were seeking. Add to this the fact that you share the same genetic code and the same brew of hormones that in the animal kingdom would encourage you to lock horns with him rather than embrace him and you can see that as a relationship it has a few obstacles to overcome.

From my own perspective, it's hard in any exploration of a father who, because of his success and accompanying fame, has provided me with a very comfortable childhood and a life of privilege not to end up sounding peevish, attention-seeking and opportunist if I make any kind of negative comment about him as a person or as a parent. There is a risk it will read like the sort of self-serving and self-pitying account that appears in a Sunday tabloid accompanied by a picture of the put-upon offspring looking forlorn and downtrodden on a park bench but off camera feeling quite perky as they cash the cheque for the exclusive serialisation rights.

I thought long and hard about whether I should add my experiences to this examination of the relationship between fathers and sons because I didn't want to hijack what is an extraordinary tale of a man, my grandfather, who really had something to moan about and chose not to and just got on with life the best way he could. On the other hand it would seem perverse for my dad and me to co-write a book about his relationship with his father and then not take the opportunity to examine ours and see how and if the title of the book applied to us.

My dad lives in me through a talent for writing and a love of reading that he has passed on to all three boys. I am also, like him, interested in the inner workings of others, the hidden truth behind the public face, probably for the same reason he is. I am also a natural loner and can, like him, close myself off to others. But shyness is not something we share, because the bulk of my personality is courtesy of my mum, with all its convoluted and unpredictable nature. I think this particular genetic mix is the reason why my dad and I have worked successfully together for over fifteen years and, despite the odd occasion when murder was contemplated on both sides, it has been a successful, enjoyable and, for me, revealing relationship.

Me showing early signs of being camera-shy.

I say revealing because it gave me an opportunity to try and understand the man who had for many years whilst I was growing up been the cause of some unease and unhappiness in my life. As I have said, he was never violent or abusive, just a man who was difficult to warm to. For most of my childhood he was a distant figure who would only appear at meal times, when he would proceed to issue diktats and less-than-complimentary observations on length of hair, performance at school and sporting prowess, and being the eloquent man that he is, these bon mots seldom missed the mark. Though his comments were mostly directed at my two brothers, they had the effect of creating a charged and unpleasant atmosphere.

Once during a particularly fractious exchange over the dinner table, after precociously reading Aldous Huxley's *Brave New World* and thinking I understood it, I suggested Dad had outlived his usefulness to society and was a prime candidate for euthanasia, which had the effect of stopping him mid-flow and resulted in him leaving the room in high dudgeon whilst the rest of the family looked on in disbelief at my audacity. It was my Kirk Douglas moment but, looking back, I'm not proud. It was the thoughtless throwaway comment of an immature child in love with his library and I'm sure to my dad it was very hurtful.

Despite this moment of rebellion, for the most part we were all too scared to stick our heads above the parapet, and therefore in general he was a figure who inspired disquiet and anxiety, and we looked for protection to our mum, who in turn, as has been revealed, was not emotionally equipped to be a strong barrier and could look to no one near her for help. It made for, on occasion, an unhappy home. And yet my father adored my mother, still does, and loved us as his sons. He just didn't seem to know how to show us. I was not terrorised by him; I just found him forbidding and distant and was unhappy that he couldn't find a better way of being close to me, couldn't just be proud without the caveats.

To be fair to him, our relationship was also coloured by an accompanying issue, over which he had no control. This concerned difficulties with my self-esteem that stemmed from growing up in a long shadow and wondering where and how you'll find your place in the sun without being compared or having where you are or what you achieve always accompanied by the stain or accusation of nepotism. It's not his fault he's very good at what he does and a lot of people like watching him do it. And as I write this there is also a small voice in the back of my head that keeps saying, 'First World problems.'

Working with him over the last few years has probably been akin to his experience of collaborating on this book. As he has with his father, I have learnt more about him as a man and have come to understand him, warts and all, and in a sense to finally outgrow his dominating presence. As we revealed in the last chapter, the route into the book was opened by revisiting some of his interviews when he asked people about their fathers. Apart from being amazed that one or two of those people didn't take inspiration from Lord Carnarvon and mete out their revenge with a stiletto blade,

I also came across one that personally interested me. It was with **Jane Fonda,** where she finally revealed the truth behind one of the most complicated and dysfunctional father-and-child relationships.

Her father was the Hollywood icon Henry Fonda, who my dad had interviewed years before his celebrated daughter appeared on the show. She had just written an autobiography that was a searingly honest account of the effects on her personal life of her 'father issues' and the way she had finally put them to bed. I can in no way claim that the fallout from my difficulties had the same devastating effect on me as Jane Fonda's did on her, but I could see strong echoes of my early life in the way she had come to understand what was happening between her and her father.

MICHAEL: In many ways, to somebody like myself who grew up watching your father and yourself too and forming opinions, as you do from the silver screen, it's quite a shocking book.

JANE FONDA: How so?

MICHAEL: Take your father as an example. To me, he epitomised on the screen that wonderful all-American hero: a lovely, gentle, charismatic man. Yet he comes across in your book as a kind of a cruel man in many

211

ways: cruel to you, a bad father, cold, distant.

JANE FONDA: Cold rather than cruel. But you can also feel how much I loved him, right?

MICHAEL: Of course, I mean you spent all of your life trying to please him.

JANE FONDA: 'The disease to please.'

MICHAEL: Is that what it is?

JANE FONDA: Men understand it just as well as women. It happens when you are growing up. You feel or are sometimes made to feel that you are not good enough, that in order to be loved you have to be perfect, and of course we're not meant to be perfect, right? God is perfect; we're meant to be complete. But you turn yourself into a pretzel to please. It happened that with me it was my father I was trying to please, and it doesn't stop when you grow up. It became the men I was with, all of whom I was sure were totally different to my father, but underneath there was the same issue, which is that they didn't know, nor did I, how to be intimate. And that is very universal.

MICHAEL: But what was the problem with your father, that he had lacked this intimacy with you, that he was distant, he was disapproving? Is that the fact?

JANE FONDA: Well, it's partly generational. How many of you saw *On Golden Pond*? Well, that relationship in the movie, between me, Chelsea, and Norman, my father, played by my father, was very parallel to the real-life relationship.

MICHAEL: But did he see the parallels?

JANE FONDA: I just assumed that he did, but he never told me he did.

MICHAEL: So never in all the time that you were with him, that you knew him, did he ever give you the seal of approval, so to speak?

JANE FONDA: He did, on your programme.

MICHAEL: Well, he did, this is the point, in 1975, and you didn't know about that, did you?

JANE FONDA: No.

MICHAEL: He said that you were the most remarkable actress he had ever seen and that there was a moment in *Klute* where you did something and he said, 'I can't do that.' Now, he never told you that?

JANE FONDA: No, no.

MICHAEL: Isn't that strange, though, weird, that he will tell me but won't tell you?

JANE FONDA: We all, or many of us, know parents who are wonderful with strangers, especially after a few drinks, but in the living room or the bedroom with their intimates they don't know how to show up, they don't know how to love. And you can learn, but the generation of my father really didn't think that that was something you . . . well, he didn't learn.

MICHAEL: The other thing that is extraordinary is the way that your father, who has cast this long shadow over your life . . .

JANE FONDA: It's all part of 'I've got to be perfect to be loved'.

MICHAEL: That's right. Your father didn't approve of the way you looked, so *you* didn't approve of the way you looked, so you became bulimic.

JANE FONDA: And anorexic, for twenty-five years.

MICHAEL: For twenty-five years, and none of the people who you were with knew about it?

JANE FONDA: Of course not. If you are an addict, which is what food addiction is, just like alcohol and drugs, if you are an addict, you are always going to be attracted to people who are also addicts because you can be intuitively quite sure they will never notice because they are too busy with their own addiction. Maybe the perfect man for me crossed my path at some point in my life, who was actually capable of intimacy, and you know what I would have done? Fled in terror. Addicts are attracted to addicts so that no one will call them on their issues. And when I got healthy . . . I'm alone. But I'm not, I'm here with you, I'm very happy and I have grandkids and children.

If I've learnt one thing from this book it is that no one's bad behaviour is totally exonerated by Philip Larkin's 'coastal shelf' explanation, but it does go a long way towards explaining why a father's love can sometimes be so inarticulately and hurtfully expressed. For my dad it cannot have been easy being a son to a mother like my gran.

She was many things but she wasn't by nature a patient nurturer, and I can well imagine that she was at times a hard and unforgiving taskmaster with my dad and would have delivered excoriating speeches, just as he did at our dinner table in later life, on his performance and behaviour while his father sat by watching, unable to step in, because of his personality and his devotion to his wife. She was 'tough love' personified, and a young mind is a ball of putty and none of us can ever truly escape the imprint of our past. It also cannot have been easy being an only child, which is poor preparation for learning the essential lesson that the world doesn't revolve around you and that your actions have an impact upon others who share the same space as you.

The French coined a rather chauvinistic phrase to explain any problem affecting a man, mainly of the romantic variety, of 'cherchez la femme', or 'look for the woman'. Other than the fact that it was the central theme of *Farewell, My Lovely*, a novel featuring the hardbitten gumshoe Philip Marlowe by Raymond Chandler, one of my father's favourite authors, it is also, in the wider sense, an apposite phrase to employ when you are trying to understand my father: 'Cherchez la mère.' She, in my view, for better and worse, is the defining influence upon him and because of that the inevitable conclusion is that the title of this book is a misnomer.

My dad is much more his mother's son, and he shares with her some of the traits that made her a difficult woman to get on with, but also those which blessed him with an enquiring, avaricious mind that makes him encyclopaedic in his knowledge of subjects as wide-ranging as art, music, movies and literature, plus the personality to be a force of nature if he wants something done. His father was a man he marvelled at, adored and simply hoped he could become. He told Piers Morgan his father was a better man than him, but he perhaps doesn't realise that he carries within him much more of John William Parkinson than he knows.

*Dad with Nick, the youngest googly bowler in
the northern hemisphere.*

He is kind, generous, compassionate, funny when he
remembers to smile and a weaver of outlandish tales that he
insists, just like his father did, are true. But we all have traits
that are very much our own and, whether they are created
by a chance meeting of a DNA strand or by regular meetings with parents over the kitchen table, those facets of our

character are what define us as an individual, and for many reading this, my dad's will be surprising.

He is, for a man who has spent years in the spotlight, someone who shuns it in his everyday life. He is shy and hates being the centre of attention, which is why at every social event he sends my mum in first like a social Panzer Division. He is at heart a solitary man who makes and needs few friends, and though he has many talents, he lacks real self-confidence, which is often the case with gifted people in any area of the creative arts.

Yet, despite the lottery into which all sons are born, the differences in my dad's and grandfather's characters, the yawning gulf between their opportunities and expectations, what shines through is a strong bond and love between them. My dad's relationship with his father is less Philip Larkin and more Pop Larkin. As he says, he struck it lucky. It was a relationship that nurtured and comforted him and stays with him to this day.

The loss of his father was such a devastating blow because it was a treasured relationship cut short by the uncaring actions of his father's employers, and it was one that because of the demands of a miner's job and the sometimes cloying grip of his mother's love, he could never quite get enough of as a child. On an emotional and physical level, he still misses him terribly, which is why tears are never far away when talk moves to John William Parkinson. That is the true meaning of this particular father-and-son tale.

The mere fact that this book has been published is the fulfilment of a hope that when my dad first read what I have contributed he would see it for what it is and where it came from. In return for being given free rein to express my particular viewpoint of him and his relations with his parents, I've light-heartedly suggested that this could be the beginning of a series of books in the style of that wonderful Michael Apted-created documentary series *7 Up*. In my version, rather than following the lives of seven strangers as they grow into adulthood and beyond, we would allow the latest generation of Parkinsons to produce an audit of the previous generation's parenting skills. It's only fair, given what I've written, but I am slightly worried by the enthusiasm my dad showed for this idea and the keenness expressed by my children to be the authors of the sequel.

The title *Like Father, Like Son* started as a statement, became a question and ended up being discarded as a way of summing up a life. We are all an amalgam of our parents; we are all a product of that time-immemorial wrestling match of nature versus nurture. It is a roll of the dice as to how the brew concocts itself and we have little control over how it shapes the way we are. Which is why this book is as much about forgiveness as it is about love.

As I've already said, Larkin, Philip not Pop, has a point: it's not totally your parents' fault. They're only passing on what was done to them and, as long as it doesn't involve deprivation, excessive violence or worse, what they need is understanding, not blame. To understand really does lead to forgiveness, particularly in my case when, like all things that erode over time, the 'coastal shelf' has lost its jagged edges as prosperity and opportunity pass down the family line and life becomes simpler to navigate. It is too easy to sit in judgement from a comfortable position created by people who lived lives in hard, uncompromising times. They did what was best with what they had and the recipients of their sacrifices should try and look beyond their rough edges and appreciate them. It's the sort of relationship the miners wanted with the outside world but never really achieved. Appreciation not opprobrium.

The Bard, our great chronicler of the human psyche, is also right when he says the fault lies in 'ourselves' because a certain degree of self-determination and responsibility goes a long way towards making up for the perceived parental deficiencies in your life. As the Bible says, 'Physician, heal thyself'. Larkin's prescription to avoid the inevitable pain of bungled parenting is to remain childless. I think, as this book testifies, both sides of the equation would miss out on too much by doing that. I know from my perspective I would have, because I have had the privilege of being a son to two extraordinary people.

They have given me priceless gifts both genetically and through their love. They have lived their lives under the distorting glare of fame, but their feet have only left the ground a couple of times and the family has been central to all that they did. Life with them is never boring and they have never been a burden to me, and never will be, no matter what the future throws at them.

But that's enough from me, I'll let my dad have the last word – as per usual!

CHAPTER 9

THE LAST WORD

INTERVIEWER: *Would I be right in thinking that if you ever do write a novel, it will hark back to Barnsley and the old days?*

MICHAEL PARKINSON: *I've got a novel in my head. I know the title and I know the cover. It's called* Like Father, Like Son.

Club magazine interview, 1971

A family story.

THIS WAS ALWAYS GOING TO be an unusual book for me to write. I have never been renowned as a relationship counsellor – not much call for them growing up in Cudworth, or indeed Yorkshire – nor am I very adept or comfortable with the touchy-feely side of life. So it is somewhat inevitable that it would be Mike, coming from a generation more at ease with not necessarily diving but at least dipping a small toe into the whirlpool of familial relationships and emotions, who would by necessity take the lead in attempting to unravel the message and unscramble the picture that is contained between the lines of the articles I wrote about my father and see the boy I was and the man I have become.

It's been fascinating and moving to work alongside Mike in creating this book about my father. But he is also right when he says it has not been an easy task. Given that it is essentially about love and was written in the most extraordinary circumstances of a lockdown created by a pandemic, I

225

wanted to subtitle the book, with apologies to Gabriel García Márquez, 'Love in the Time of Corona'. You might think that the strictures of a national lockdown would be manna from heaven to the struggling scribe in his frozen garret. This period of environmental quiet and the chance for 'twitching' or contemplative star-gazing, the ceasing of the hurly-burly and the consequent lack of demands upon your time would surely release a flood of creativity, the words dripping from pen or computer, or in my case antique type-writer, like gobbets of golden nectar from flowering plants on a late spring morning.

Fat chance.

Let me tell you, this has been one of the most difficult books I have ever written, notwithstanding the fact that it is a book of memories and, whilst the mental library is still intact and regularly dusted, someone has recently nicked the card index and thrown all the books on the floor. The truth is, trying to motivate oneself to write anything during this awful pandemic has been tough. Being in an age in which this silent hunter is going for the jugular, when actual news is replaced by recita-tions of the number of dead and infected, reminders that this is our lot for the foreseeable future and forecasts that when we emerge it will probably be to the dying ashes of a world econ-omy does not an inspired writer make.

One of my favourite photos of Mary.

That is why it is essential to be married to a woman of Irish descent who is both practical, full of common sense and quite the funniest person I have ever had the pleasure to meet. She is also, if I ever look like taking to my chaise longue in a fit of creative ennui, a dab hand at issuing motivational speeches that range in tone, content and colourful language from Mahatma Gandhi to Sir Alex Ferguson.

Leaning for support on my co-author,
business partner and youngest son.

It is also essential to have a co-writer with a brain thirty-odd years younger and the energy and drive that comes with that. As he has with other recent books on Muhammad Ali and George Best, my youngest son, Mike, has provided the most essential service any writer can hope for: to stop talking about it, fretting about the deadline and quibbling about the number of words and actually start writing the bloody thing, as well as providing the foundations and structure upon which I can festoon my pearls of wisdom. He is to me what

Riddle was to Sinatra, and I can think of no bigger compliment, except that both of us could play a better cover drive than Ol' Blue Eyes and Nelson.

The seemingly prescient quote at the beginning of the chapter comes from an interview I did with the now-defunct *Club* magazine. It was sent to me in the early days of writing this book by my aforementioned publisher Roddy Bloomfield. Given that the magazine in question had all the sensibilities of a downmarket gentlemen's club, complete with pole-dancing room, the full interview was a vivid example of what a prat I made of myself when I tried to be one of the lads. However, the passage about the proposed novel was a timely reminder that this book didn't exist solely in Roddy's imagination and was an encouragement that what we were embarking upon was in fact fulfilling a lifetime ambition.

The difference is that back then I was seeing it as a modern-day, funny version of *How Green Was My Valley*, but what Mike and I have created has, in my humble opinion, far outstripped anything that was in my mind at that stage of my life. This book is an honest assessment of a family's relationship with each other, seen through the prism of their shared love for one man, and although at times it makes uncomfortable reading for me, it would have been dishonest if we had tried to gloss over the sharp edges that exist in any family as they grow together. The enduring strength of us as a family, the fact we are all still talking to each other, is an indication that the rough and tumble of our early days has not taken too much of a toll.

It has also been a chance to examine what grief has done to me. I am at peace about the loss of my mother. I am well aware of the shortcomings that Mike has revealed and the sometimes negative effect she had on me and other members of the family, but she was a remarkable woman and remains one of the most important and potent influences in my early life. Her insistence that I read voraciously and develop my writing was no burden to me, as I enjoyed doing both, but how she laboured to improve my father's situation was a thing to behold. I remember sitting at the dining table doing my homework and being aware of my mother sitting next to my father, trying to help him with his reading and writing skills so that he could get through the deputies' exam. He was an unwilling, difficult pupil as he had left school with basic literacy skills and, as has already been said, he didn't want to put himself above the men who were his friends and trusted workmates. But she never gave up, never relented, and because of what she did for both of us I can feel nothing but gratitude and love for her. But ever since my father died, I have been in the grip of a grief which has in many ways paralysed me and made it impossible for me to come to terms with his loss.

I didn't realise that grief physically hurt until I lost him. I didn't realise that grief can linger for this long and disprove the adage that 'time is a great healer'. But the process of finally telling the story of me and my father's relationship in the way we have and reading of the affection he is held in by all branches of the family has caused me to feel nothing but pride and gratitude that I was his son. I hope and I pray that in some way this book may help me to be finally at peace with the loss of him.

He died well before his time, but at least he got to see me make my mark as the host of *Parkinson*. He loved coming to the show and moved effortlessly around the Green Room, chatting to anyone who would listen, engaging Hollywood stars and waitresses with the same easy, unaffected manner. Everyone who met him felt they had known him for a long time.

It was good to see my parents enjoying my success, knowing how important their role had been in setting me free to follow my dreams. I tried at every opportunity to thank them. We bought them a lovely cottage at the foot of the Chiltern Hills and sent them on holidays to places like Lanzarote, Madeira and the Greek islands. My father didn't travel well, however, and tales of his mishaps abroad became legendary in the Parkinson family canon. One of the most memorable was a cruise on an ocean liner, as I recounted in my autobiography.

I bought my dad a white linen jacket and black bow tie, which would be suitable if they were invited to the captain's table. I knew they would receive an invitation, because we had arranged for it to happen. It arrived for the third night of their voyage, a cocktail party followed by dinner with the captain.

My father was dressed before my mother, so he said he would go ahead and see her at the cocktail party. Attired in white jacket and bow tie, he set off. When my mother arrived twenty minutes later, she was horrified to see him standing by the door, just about buried in mink wraps and other garments.

Apparently, he had been dithering at the door when a couple mistook him for the doorman and handed him their coats. From that point on, the longer he stood there, the more garments were deposited in his arms until, when my mother arrived, he was literally buried in fur.

'Gormless,' said my mother. 'That's what he is, gormless.'

His great ambition was to go to Australia to follow an Ashes series. He greatly admired the Aussies, believing they were antipodean Yorkshiremen, part of the same tribe, loving beer, plain speaking and cricket. When I first visited Australia and went to the Sydney Cricket Ground and saw the Hill and the lovely old pavilion, I knew what he meant and what he had missed.

He formed a special bond with Mary, filling the gap in her life caused by her father's early death, and becoming her mentor and her champion. She, in turn, felt a deep love for him.

When he was very unwell and in hospital, it was to Mary he confessed his deepest fear. 'I don't want to die here,' he said.

So she brought him home and for a month or more he lay in palliative care, while we watched his life ebbing away like a disappearing tide.

He died as he had lived, without making a fuss.

When the undertakers came for him, they brought him downstairs in a blue rubber bag and he looked so small and insignificant I turned my head away. In that moment I accommodated his death by pretending it hadn't happened.

I began to drink even more than normal, which was to say, a lot. The more I drank, the more depressed I became. I went to see a psychiatrist, who probed away but didn't tell me anything I didn't already know. My drinking didn't interfere with my work. I didn't drink for twenty-four hours before a show and never ever on the day itself, at least not until the show had ended.

It was Mary who caused me to change.

She said to me one day, 'You know the worst thing about you and drink?'

I asked what she thought it was.

'It makes you ugly,' she said.

Her words rang in my brain ever after and, without ever causing me to become teetotal, made me forever cautious of further excess.

One day, about two years after my father died, I came across a picture of him as a young man, a group photograph of the village cricket team outside the pavilion on the ground where I first saw him play. He looked eager, athletic and handsome, and the image broke the dam of my grief and I started crying. I cried for an hour or so, tears of love and regret, of pride and guilt – remembering him with all the love, joy and laughter he gave to us when he lived.

John William Parkinson, the reason for this book, spent a large part of his life in the darkness but was determined to spread light wherever he went. He touched us all profoundly and left his mark on each one of us. He lives on in me in ways I don't realise; in Mary when she takes off down another cul de sac; in my eldest boy Andrew when pursuing a lost cause on a sports field; in my middle boy Nick whenever a party is in full swing; in my youngest Mike in the way that he always approaches any task or challenge with a sense of shining optimism.

He even lives on in those he never met. Recently, my youngest granddaughter, Sofia, surprisingly asked me, given her usual musical taste, if I had heard of the singing group The Ink Spots, because she loves their version of 'Whispering Grass'. Little did she know it was her great grandfather's favourite song too, and I wondered if it was him saying a quick hello through the next generation.

Rest in peace father, father-in-law, grandfather, miner, proud Yorkshireman who's currently opening the bowling with a smile on his face armed with a frayed tennis ball and the help of a strong crosswind blowing over the Elysian Fields and telling anyone who'll listen just how proud he is of his only child. You never know, if we meet again, I might have finally stopped playing the cut shot before the chrysanthemums have flowered. Thank you for what you did for us all and, never mind me, we all miss you.

PHOTOGRAPHIC ACKNOWLEDGEMENTS

The author and publisher would like to thank the following for permission to reproduce photographs:

Dinozzo/123RF; The Francis Frith Collection; KGPA Ltd/Alamy Stock Photo; The Francis Frith Collection; Daily Herald Archive/SSPL/Getty Images; Haywood Magee/Picture Post/Hulton Archive/Getty Images; Sasha/ Getty Images; Central Press/Getty Images; Topical Press Agency/Getty Images; Hulton-Deutsch Collection/ CORBIS/Corbis via Getty Images; PA Images; Ken McKay/Shutterstock; Victor Watts/Shutterstock; Sunday Times/News Licensing.

Other photographs are from private collections.